The Normal Way of Fruit-bearing and Shepherding for the Building Up of the Church

Witness Lee

Living Stream Ministry

Anaheim, CA • www.lsm.org

First Edition, July 2005.

ISBN 0-7363-2910-2

Published by

Living Stream Ministry
2431 W. La Palma Ave., Anaheim, CA 92801 U.S.A.
P. O. Box 2121, Anaheim, CA 92814 U.S.A.

Printed in the United States of America

05   06   07   08   09   10   11   /   9   8   7   6   5   4   3   2   1

CONTENTS

PREFACE

This book is composed of messages given by Brother Witness Lee in weekly training meetings from December 1974 to February 1975 in Anaheim, California. These messages were not reviewed by the speaker.

CHAPTER ONE

SERVING THE LORD BY CARING FOR PEOPLE

Scripture Reading: 1 John 5:16a; Exo. 21:5-6; Isa. 50:4-5; Rom. 12:11

THE NEED TO BE TRAINED FOR OUR SERVICE

Many Christians throughout the centuries have held to one of two extremes concerning our service to the Lord. Certain "spiritual" persons insist that to serve the Lord is absolutely a matter of life. They say that since we have life, we will grow in our service, so there is no need of any training. Those at the other extreme insist that we must receive schooling in order to serve. In 1958 I was invited to a Christian meeting in London that was considered to be very spiritual. The leading ones turned all the meetings over to me for an entire month, including not only the conference meetings but also the regular meetings. Before I left, they asked me to have another time with them for questions and answers. The main question that night was from one of the young people, who had heard that we had many trainings in Taiwan. In that place of meeting in London, however, they did not have any kind of training. Their feeling was that to serve the Lord is a matter of life, and as long as they had the growth in life, they did not need training. I told them, "When I was young, my mother sent me to school specifically to learn English. However, even today my speech is too poor. A small child can speak English better than I can, even though I began to learn English long before he was born. I was trained to write and to read silently. I was trained to know grammar, and I may know grammar better than you do, but I was not adequately trained to speak. We cannot train a dog to speak English, because a dog does not have the English-speaking life. Only human beings can speak the human language. Still, we cannot say that as long as we have the human life, we can grow in this life to be able to speak English. We all have the human life, but you speak English well, and I speak it poorly. This is because you received a training that I did not."

I continued by using the example of learning to fly an airplane. I said, "We cannot train a monkey to pilot an airplane, because the monkey life is not good for this purpose. Only the human life can do this, but this does not mean that as long as we have the human life we can all pilot an airplane. If we believe this, we will damage many lives." I concluded, "Dear ones, by this we can see that we need the proper life plus the proper training. We should not insist on either extreme. Yes, we need life; without life we cannot carry out the spiritual things. However, this does not mean that as long as we have life we need nothing more. In addition to the proper life, we still need the proper training and practice."

The Apostle Paul's Realization of the Need for Training

Near the end of his life Paul wrote 1 and 2 Timothy and Titus, the three "pastoral" Epistles, because he realized from his experience that there was the need for training. Paul learned many things from his experience. For example, in the first stage of his ministry, Paul said that it is better to be like him and remain single and that to be married is a cause of troubles (1 Cor. 7:7-8, 32-34). At that time Paul had received a revelation, but he did not yet have much experience in the church life. Later he told Timothy that widows under sixty years of age should be encouraged to marry again (1 Tim. 5:9, 14). By that time he had seen some who made a vow to the Lord to love Him as single ones but eventually fell into fornication. These experiences taught Paul something further. In the early books of Paul's writing, such as Romans and 1 and 2 Thessalonians, we do not see the consideration of training, but his later books—especially 1 and 2 Timothy and Titus—are filled with the concept of training and discipline. He said, "The things which you have heard from me through many witnesses, these commit to faithful men, who will be competent to teach others also" (2 Tim. 2:2). Paul had taught and trained Timothy, and now he charged him to train others with what he had been trained by Paul.

Likewise, in his earlier writings Paul said nothing about the qualifications of elders, deacons, and deaconesses, but in the later Epistles he pointed out all these qualifications. A man does not merely grow into qualifications; qualifications come from training. Therefore, training is very scriptural. In the past twelve years I have spoken much against many traditional and unscriptural teachings of Christianity. Because of this, some may say, "Brother Lee, did you not tell us that we need life, not teaching?" What I said is that we do not need mere doctrinal teaching. After we receive life, we do not need teachings in letter, but we do need training. Paul learned something from his experiences. Likewise, according to our study of Paul's writings and according to our experience in the past years, there is the need for training.

Watchman Nee's Burden for a Formal Training

When I was with Brother Watchman Nee, he would often say, "Witness, we need the training." Brother Nee was saved in 1920, and he began the work for the Lord in 1922. After a number of years, he realized that there was the need of training. In 1936 he bought a portion of land and built a center for the purpose of training. However, in August of the next year Japan invaded Shanghai, and the building was destroyed. Three years after that, in 1940, he rented a place in Shanghai to begin the first formal, year-round training. Every week there was one meeting for training, and many persons remained there all week to wait for that one training meeting. Besides this, we also attended all the church meetings. For the whole year we heard three messages a week, one in the training meeting and two in the church meetings on the Lord's Day and on Wednesday night.

After the war, the work of the Lord spread widely throughout China, and Brother Nee returned to his ministry. He told me, "Witness, I will not carry out my ministry in the way that I did in the past. What I will do now is simply take care of the training. After 1948 he no longer took care of the church meetings. He stayed on the mountain with many lodgings in order to train people. These trainings were selective; not everyone was allowed to attend. The first period of training in 1948 was about six months long, and the second period in 1949 was also six months. He charged me to care for the work and fight the battle elsewhere. I was to send the believers as the good material to him to be trained, and after their training he would send them back to the churches. By this, I realized that in the first stage of the Lord's work there is not much need for training, but after the churches have been raised up and there is the responsibility of caring for the serving ones, we need the training.

After this time I was sent to the island of Taiwan. There we began the work in 1949, and in 1952 we began the training. This training was also selective. I did not train all the saints but trained only the serving ones, including the co-workers, elders, deacons, deaconesses, and all the promising ones. Every year we held a conference for one week to ten days with a large congregation of two or three thousand, which grew to four or five thousand. Each week we would meet on Tuesday through Friday in the mornings and evenings, and in the afternoons we would have practice. On Saturday the trainees would return to their local churches to serve throughout the weekend, on Monday they would come back to the training, and on Tuesday morning we would begin again. This went on for four to six months a year. The work in Taiwan depended mostly upon this training.

Our Lack of Training Exposed
in the Shortage of Proper Leading Ones
in the Migrations

When the work began in the United States, we were in the first stage. On the one hand, there was no need for a training, and on the other hand, I did not have time to do the training. I needed more time for travel and other matters. This is the reason that before 1970 we did not have a formal training. However, beginning from 1968 we had an informal training. A great need for the informal training was related to migrations.

After our summer conference in Los Angeles on Bonnie Brae Street in 1964, many were excited and wanted to go out to "take the country" in the way of migration. I did not feel that this was the time to go out. An army cannot go to fight without training. This only exposes them to the enemy. However, some still wanted to go out, and I did not insist that they stay. All who went out, though, returned in defeat by the end of the year. The following year we moved to Elden hall, and after two more years, in 1967, some still longed to go out to establish the local churches in other places. However, I still felt that the time was not ripe and that the migration should wait a few more years. Finally, in the fall of 1969, there was a migration from Yorba Linda to Seattle and from three small cities in Texas to Houston. Then in 1970 further migrations took place. Without exception, the first stage of all the migrations was a success. Although in the six years from 1964 to 1970 we had not had a formal training, a proper leadership had been produced among us. Wherever the migrations went, they went with a proper leadership; therefore, they were a success.

On the contrary, there were more migrations in 1973, but almost none was a success. This is because we were short of the proper leading ones. After remaining in the new localities for a year, many of the saints could not go on, but they dared not go back. They simply remained there in a suffering way. Eventually, many who had gone out consolidated into churches in certain major cities. This shortage of the proper leadership exposes our further need for training. At that time I went to the Lord very much concerning my ministry. The Lord has made it clear that my ministry in this country to serve the saints should be different from what it was in the previous twelve years. The previous twelve years was the first stage among us. I needed to travel for the setting up of the churches. Now there are thirty-five churches in this country, and my time and strength do not allow me to visit them all. Among the approximately five thousand saints in the Lord's recovery, there is not the adequate leadership. Even in Anaheim alone there are enough saints to become two churches, but we do not have the proper leadership to carry this out. Therefore, there is now the need of a continual training. The

Lord has shown me that from now on I must spend all my time in the ministry for the training.

The training is not for acquiring mere knowledge. It is for practice and the proper discipleship. The training builds us up in the growth of life, in character, and in dealing with the natural disposition. Character is our disposition plus our habit. We need a change in our character. Even more deeply, the training touches our natural disposition. Strictly speaking, it is not our nature but our disposition that needs to be touched and dealt with. If we are trained in this way even for only a few months, we will see a difference.

THE PURPOSE OF OUR SERVICE
BEING TO MINISTER LIFE TO OTHERS

The first point for our training is to realize that in the church service we do not do anything in the way of organization. The church is an organism, and what an organism needs is life. Therefore, our church service is mainly for ministering life to others. Even the arranging of chairs and the cleaning of restrooms are not for themselves; they are for ministering life. In ushering, clerical work, and any aspect of the church service, we must do everything to minister life to others. Of course, it is good for us to do things in a proper way. Not doing things well can be a frustration, but this does not mean that merely doing a good job is to have the proper service. In worldly religious organizations it is sufficient to do the jobs well, but in the church the main thing we need is the ministry of life. Even if we cannot do things very well, but by His mercy we minister life to others, the service is still successful. The main matter is to minister life to others.

Some may say that it is not we but the Lord Jesus who is the Life-giver. However, there is at least one verse in the New Testament that says we can give life to the weaker ones. First John 5:16a says, "If anyone sees his brother sinning a sin not unto death, he shall ask and he will give life to him." *Life* here in Greek is not *bios,* the physical life; it is *zoe,* the spiritual life. This verse does not mean that if we pray for the brother's sickness, we can impart physical life to him. It is that we give him *zoe,* the spiritual life. We have the privilege of giving life to the weaker ones in order to swallow up their death. Many saints are not sick physically, but they are sick spiritually. They need us to pray for them and to give them life. We all need to be trained and to practice to take care of the weaker ones who are short of life and sick spiritually. In the churches it is often the case that death, rather than life, spreads from mouth to mouth. Therefore, there is the need of some stronger ones to minister life to stop the spread of death and to swallow up death. This is the main purpose of the service in the church.

The best opportunity for us to minister life to others is in the service groups. Many saints who have a heart for the Lord have been placed into these groups under the care of the responsible ones. The leading ones in the service should not care merely for doing things properly. The main thing they must do is care in life for all the ones who serve in the groups. They must help the saints not primarily to carry out the service; rather, they should fellowship with them and minister life to them so that they may grow. If the leading ones do this, spontaneously all the saints will do the same for others. Then the entire church will be under the care of the proper ministry of life.

CONSECRATING OURSELVES ANEW TO THE LORD FOR THE SERVICE AND TRAINING

In order for us to minister life to others, we must do at least four things. First, we need an adequate contact with the Lord. We must all purposely go to the Lord, not to pray for other things but simply to spend time with Him. We need to be like the purchased slave in Exodus 21. Verse 5 says, "If the servant plainly says, I love my master, my wife, and my children; I will not go out free." After six years of service the slave was free to leave, but if he loved his master, he would not go out. Moreover, while he had been in his master's house, he received a wife and had children. In type, the wife and children are the church with all the saints. We have not only the Master but also the church and all the saints as our family. We love our Lord, the church, and all the saints. We should tell the Lord, "Lord, I wish to stay. I can go out freely, but I will not. I love You. I love my wife, the church, and I love my children, the saints. I do not want to miss You, Lord, and neither do I want to miss Your church and all the saints. I want to remain here to be Your bondslave."

Verse 6 says, "Then his master shall bring him to God and shall bring him to the door or to the doorpost, and his master shall bore his ear through with an awl; and he shall serve him forever." In type, to have our ear bored is to open our ear. To be a good serving one does not depend upon our feet, our hands, or our eyes. It depends upon our open ear. To be a proper slave, we need an open ear, not to speak, do, or walk but to listen. We must not be as instructors but as the instructed, not as teachers but as learners. We all need to pray this way: "Lord, I love You, I love Your church, and I love the saints. I will never go out. Therefore, bore my ear; open my ear that I may listen to You. I do not want to be a teacher. I am a listener and a learner." Isaiah 50 is a prophetic word describing the Lord Jesus while He was on the earth. Verses 4 and 5 say, "The Lord Jehovah has given me / The tongue of the instructed, / That I should know how to sustain the weary with a word. / He awakens me morning by morning; / He awakens my ear / To hear as an instructed one. / The Lord Jehovah has opened my ear; / And I was not rebellious, / Nor did I turn back." One who has life and the timely word from the Lord can speak the timely word to sustain the weary ones. This is to minister life to the weary and weak ones. We must all go to the Lord first to consecrate ourselves anew to serve Him in the church and to participate in the service and in the training.

BEING DEALT WITH BY THE LORD UNDER HIS LIGHT

Second, we must learn in the presence of the Lord to be dealt with by Him. We may say, "Lord, here I am. I know that I am not fitting and useful. I am natural, wild, and raw; I have never been 'cooked,' processed, by You. I am even sinful, worldly, and fleshly. Lord, in order to use me as Your bondslave, You must deal with me. I need Your dealing. I need Your 'cooking.' Lord, I open myself to You, but I do not depend on my opening; I depend upon Your exposing. Bring me into Your light. Shine over me, shine within me, and shine through me thoroughly that I may be fully exposed." We all need such a prayer. It is better to pray in this way by ourselves. In doing other things we should not be individualistic, but in this kind of prayer it is better to do it individually. We should spend an hour or more in the presence of the Lord for this purpose, checking with Him again and again until we get through, and nothing further needs to be exposed.

PICKING UP A BURDEN TO CARE FOR PEOPLE

After we reconsecrate ourselves and deal thoroughly with the Lord, we can pick up a burden before Him. There is no need to pray particularly for a burden. Whatever burden we pick up will be the Lord's burden. We should not primarily care for business affairs. We may pick up a burden for ushering in the meetings, but the ushering itself is not our burden. Rather, our burden is to take care of people by ushering. Picking up a burden in this way will make a great difference. If we usher after having thoroughly dealt with the Lord, whenever we usher, we will minister life. There will be an outflow of life from us to others' spirits. The Holy Spirit always honors this kind of serving.

For this purpose, the Lord needs even the teenagers. I hope that the older teenagers will pick up the burden to care for those in junior high school. According to my observation, we have many ten-year-old, eleven-year-old, and twelve-year-old sisters, but there are no teenage sisters taking care of them. Therefore, we need some young sisters to give themselves for this. After their reconsecration and dealing with the Lord, they should say, "Lord, I pick up this burden. I give myself to take care of the junior high girls. This is my service. I will pick them up, and I will bear them all the way to the New Jerusalem." If some teenagers will do this, they will have the Lord's presence with them, and they will see the blessing. We cannot tell how far the Lord will go with these young ones. Perhaps by this kind of service they will become useful in the Lord's recovery in the coming years. They will be not only "big sisters" but mothers of many young ones.

We cannot appoint anyone to this position. We cannot say, "Sister, come to take care of the young girls." This will not work. Rather, they must go to the Lord and say, "Lord, here I am. I love You. You are my Master. I love the church, and I love the saints. I especially love the young girls ten through fifteen years old. I simply love them, Lord, and I would not go out free. O Lord, deal with me." A young sister may spend three nights to deal with the Lord in this way. After she is thoroughly dealt with by the Lord, she does not need to pray in a begging way, "Lord, have mercy upon me and give me a burden." She may simply say, "Lord, by Your grace I pick up the burden to care for the young girls. Lord, You must go with me." She can give the Lord such a command: "Lord, since I am picking up the burden, You must work with me." The Lord truly will honor her and go with her.

All the brothers and sisters need to pick up such a burden. The older sisters, for example, can pick up the burden to care for the older saints. No one can appoint us to this service. We must all go to the Lord, the Head of the Body, have a thorough dealing with Him, and pick up a burden. There are many categories of burdens. According to my observation, many needs are lying waste, and many useful persons are also lying waste. The useful persons must be matched to the needs. Neither I nor any leading brother can say, "Sister, you do this." That never works. Instead, we must all go to the Lord, have a thorough dealing with Him, and open our spiritual eyes to see the need. Then, without any ambition but even at the sacrifice of our whole life, whatever burden we pick up will be the Lord's will. It is worthwhile to pay the price even of our life. I was nineteen years old when I was saved. On that day I told the Lord, "Lord, even if You gave me the whole world, I would refuse it. I simply want to be poor for the Lord Jesus." If the young sisters do this, they will see the Lord's blessing. We must all pick up a burden to care for people. There is no other way to carry out the Lord's desire.

LEARNING TO BE INTERESTED IN PEOPLE

After we have a thorough dealing with the Lord and pick up a burden, we must learn to be interested in people. Because of the fall, many of us are not interested in others. We consider that whether others go to heaven or to hell is their own business. We do not care whether others grow in life, and we feel that it is sufficient for us to care for our own spiritual welfare. However, the church service requires every one of us to be involved with others. We need an interest in the Lord's people. We may illustrate this interest by the taste for certain foods. Many Chinese people are interested in Chinese cooking and have the taste to go to Chinatown. We, however, need to be interested in the Lord's people. Every day the Lord's people must be our "food" (John 4:31-34). Some older teenage sisters should say, "All the young girls between ten and fifteen years old in the church life are my food. I am interested in the young people to this extent."

However, we must not be interested in people in a natural way. Some people were born with the inclination to talk and even gossip. That is not what it means to be interested in people in a proper way. Many young ones like to talk about marriage, and many older ones like to ask concerning each others' children, grandchildren, and in-laws. We must forget about this kind of gossip. This is the natural, social way. Rather, we must be interested in people in the way of life. We should not care to ask about people's marriage, in-laws, or other matters. We are interested only in life. We should pray concerning this, and some may need to fast in prayer. We may pray, "Lord, by my birth I love to talk to people in a natural way," but others may need to pray, "Lord, I was born in a way that I do not like to talk to people. I love the brothers, and I have been in the church for ten years, but until today I still do not like to open myself to anyone." We should all pray, "Lord, burden me. I want to be fully interested in and involved with all Your dear saints, not in a natural or social way but in the way of life. Lord, I am willing to pay any price, even at the cost of my life. I love these people, and I would die for them. I want to see them saved, grow in life, and become matured."

Then we can pick up the burden for some specific persons. We should make a list of their names, always keep it in front of us, and pray for them one by one. A teenage sister may pray, "Lord, this one is still not saved. Lord, I will never be at peace until I see her saved. Lord, even for my sake You must save her." We may be too spiritual and say, "Lord, this is not for my sake." However, the Lord may say, "Because you have a genuine burden for this one, I will save her for your sake." Eventually the sister will see the little one be saved. After this she may say, "Lord, this little one is now saved, but she does not love You. I can never be satisfied with this. Do something in her so that she will love You, Lord, as I love You." Again, the sister will see the Lord answer her prayer. Likewise, the older generation must be burdened and pray in the same way. We need to be interested in people and involved with people. Then we can pick up a burden. Many in the church need our shoulders to bear them and our breast to embrace them (Exo. 28:9-12, 15-21, 29). We must love them. When they fall, we should weep, and when they rise up, we should be joyful. We must bear them as our burden. Our service is not to arrange the chairs, do the cleaning, usher, or do clerical work. These are temporary matters as the means, instruments, and channels for us to take care of people. We must all go to the Lord, pray, and pick up this burden.

CHAPTER TWO

CARING FOR PEOPLE AS NURSING MOTHERS AND EXHORTING FATHERS

Scripture Reading: 1 Thes. 2:7-8, 11; Matt. 4:19; John 21:15; S. S. 1:7-8

DEALING WITH THE LIGHT WE RECEIVE FROM THE LORD

In the previous chapter we stressed the need to go to the Lord, deal with Him, and receive light from Him to be exposed. Many Christians hope that a light from heaven would shine on them as it did on Saul of Tarsus (Acts 9:3). However, there has never been another Saul in history. We should not expect that one day the Lord will have mercy and shine His light on us in this way. The proper way to receive enlightenment is to deal with the light that we already have. We already have a certain amount of light, whether or not we are willing to obey it.

Our Need for Training to Deal with Matters Thoroughly

As proper persons, we rise up in the morning at the right time, make our bed, wash, dress, and have breakfast, and after breakfast we arrange our affairs. To behave in this way is not to be sloppy. Because of our fallen nature, however, almost every Christian is sloppy in his spiritual life. This is because no one exercises control over us. In our schooling, we have a teacher, professor, or at least a grading system to exercise control over us. Similarly, many who are sloppy in other things are not sloppy on their job because their desire not to lose their job controls them. In the spiritual life, however, no one exercises control over us in this way. The church cannot "fire" a brother for being sloppy. Therefore, we need the training. The training is not merely the teaching of the Bible or of skills for the church. The training is simply a spiritual discipline that builds us up to discipline ourselves. As seeking ones of the Lord, we must learn to discipline ourselves. Many housewives know how to keep their house clean. If they mean business as a housekeeper, they will not ignore a piece of waste paper when they see it but will throw it into the waste paper basket. Even a small piece of waste paper not picked up is a proof that someone is a sloppy housekeeper. We need to discipline ourselves in the Christian life in the same way. We should not tolerate having any matters that remain undealt with.

Dealing with the Light That We Already Have

Some may say that they do not know how to receive light from the Lord. In actuality, we already have the light. If we see a "piece of waste paper" in our being, this indicates that we have some light. However, we may not care for the light, and we may not want to be exposed. We may see many things that need to be dealt with, but we may not care to deal with them. Rather, we may claim that we do not have the light and do not know what to do. We do know what to do, but if we do not deal with what we see, we will not receive further light. Light brings in more light (Psa. 36:9). This applies even to physical things. If a good housekeeper cleans her furniture thoroughly, her eyes will be exercised to see dust that others cannot see. On the other hand, if we never clean our furniture in a thorough way, we will lose the ability to see the dust. The difference is a matter not of light but of sight. We may all be under the same light, but our sight is different. Proper sight depends much upon the exercise of our sight. Recently, I lost my sight, but this was remedied by surgery on my retina. After my surgery, due to the shortage of the exercise of my eyes, my vision remained poor. As I began to exercise my eyes more, my sight gradually increased. Strictly speaking, this improvement was due not to healing but to exercise.

It is not true that we, as persons saved, regenerated, and indwelt by the Holy Spirit, have no light, and it is also not true that we have no sight. We do have light and sight, but we may not exercise our sight to see, and we may not care for what we see. By the Lord's mercy, we may need to go to the Lord one night and say, "Lord, I will not go to sleep or do anything else. I will simply remain in Your presence until everything is cleared up, and there is no further speaking from my conscience." We do not necessarily need to say, "Lord, shine upon me." The Lord is already shining. To pray for light may simply be an excuse. We should not excuse ourselves. Rather, we should say, "Lord, I am sloppy in this matter that You have shown me. O Lord, forgive me." Following this, we can confess a second matter and ask for forgiveness and cleansing of that filthiness with the Lord's precious blood (1 John 1:9). Then we can go on to further matters. The more we go on, the more light we will receive; the more sight we exercise, the more things we will see. We will remain very busy in our prayer. We may think there are too many things to deal with, but the Lord may say that there are more to come. Perhaps after fifteen minutes we will fall to the floor repenting and weeping. If we obey a small light, that light will bring in further light, and if we obey the further light, it will bring in even greater light.

Do not wait for enlightenment. We are already in the light and under the light. This is the meaning of going to the Lord to deal thoroughly with Him. We should not say that we do not know how to clean our room or where to start. We should simply clean the spot on which we are standing. After we clean the first spot, we will see a second spot, and after we clean the second spot, right away we will see a third one. The more thoroughly we clean, the more we will see the need of cleaning. Eventually, we may need to come back to the same spot to clean it again. We thought it was clean the first time, but when we come back to it, we will see that the first cleansing was not thorough. Regrettably, though, we are too sloppy. We have listened to many messages, we appreciated them, and we said Amen. Now the light has already begun to shine on us all, and we are under the Lord's enlightenment. We simply need to obey the light, exercise our sight, and have a thorough dealing in the presence of the Lord.

BECOMING NURSING MOTHERS
AND EXHORTING FATHERS

As we pointed out in the previous chapter, the church service is not mainly for doing things but for taking care of persons. Our present training is not to build up our skill to be a leader, to usher, or to arrange chairs. I have no intention to carry out this kind of training. Chair arranging is not for chair arranging itself, and ushering is not for ushering itself. If we do a good job merely in the practical matters but do not take care of anyone, we are a failure. This is the way of a worldly corporation. Whatever we do in the church life is for the care of persons. It is easy to do practical things, but to take care of persons is much more difficult. If a sister asks us to clean her house, we may do it in half a day, but if she asks us to take care of her children, we would certainly refuse, because to do that is not "in our blood." Before a young sister is married, it may be very difficult to regulate her. After she is married and has children, however, there is no need to regulate her. Her children become very skillful regulators, and she is willing to be regulated. Previously she may have refused to do dirty jobs, but now she will happily do the dirtiest job. This is because she now has a mother's "blood." She does it because she loves her children.

First Thessalonians 2:7 says, "We were gentle in your midst, as a nursing mother would cherish her own children." To cherish is not merely to do a job or to carry out a business; it is to care for a living person. Verse 11 says, "Just as you know how we were to each one of you, as a father to his own children, exhorting you and consoling you and testifying." Paul nourished the Thessalonians as a mother and exhorted them as a father. The apostle was not a businessman or a school master. He was a nourishing mother and an exhorting father. He had an interest in people. If we do not have an interest in people, we are finished with the church service; we are not qualified to serve. We should not say that only the apostle Paul could be like this. What the apostle did is an example for all the believers. We are not apostles, but we should still be nursing mothers. Even the brothers must nourish others as a mother, and the sisters should exhort others as a father. This does not depend on our being male or a female; it depends on the kind of heart we have. A sister can have the heart of a father, and a brother can have the heart of a mother. This passage shows what the apostle Paul was in the Lord's service. He did not consider himself to be a great man. He considered himself as a small nursing mother and an exhorting, consoling father. His heart was the heart of a mother and of a father (2 Cor. 12:14-15). The heart of a mother is altogether for the care of her children, and the heart of a father is for their upbringing. Even if a mother keeps her house clean and in order, she will condemn herself if she neglects her children. To care for her children is of the first importance; to clean the house is the last. In the church service we should all have such a heart. Strictly speaking, we do not care for keeping the chairs. We care for keeping the persons. The keeping of chairs will not enter into the New Jerusalem, but the keeping of persons will go on forever.

I am afraid that too many of us in the church service care only for the practical service, not for the persons. We need the Lord's mercy to properly exercise our heart. This is a great test to us. Some of us were born in such a way that we do not care for anyone. This is according to our natural disposition. Hallelujah, we have been reborn in another way! We have been reborn, not into a natural family but into the church. This is another birth with another disposition that is absolutely different. The disposition of our new birth is one that sacrifices our self, our soul, and even our lives for the care of others.

THE TESTIMONY OF THE MISSIONARIES IN CHINA

In the latter part of the nineteenth and the first part of the twentieth centuries a number of missions sent missionaries into the field. Most of the missions tested their new applicants, but not in the way of testing only their knowledge of the Bible. Hudson Taylor was the founder of the China Inland Mission, one of the greatest mission works. One day he made an appointment for a young applicant to come for an interview. When the applicant arrived, Taylor asked him to wait for another twenty minutes. Then at the end of the twenty minutes, he sent word to the applicant to wait for another twenty minutes. At this point, the young applicant was a little offended, but since he still desired to get into this mission, he exercised his patience. A third time and a fourth time, Taylor asked the young man to wait for yet another twenty minutes. After the fourth delay, the young man was unable to tolerate it, and he walked out. Taylor said that it was right for him to leave. If he would go to China, he would have to wait many times longer for one person to be saved.

Missions such as these were the Lord's work at that time to send His gospel to the uttermost parts of the earth. When I was a small boy, I observed the situation of the missionaries. Those dear saints who went on the mission were very much disciplined by the Lord to have a heart for the heathen peoples, and it was through them—not through their preaching or teaching but through what they were—that many were saved. It is difficult to imagine what manner of patience, endurance, and attitude they expressed to those unbelieving heathen. This touched the conscience of the people, and it opened the door of the gospel.

The ancient and great country of China was extremely conservative at that time. The Boxer Movement of 1900 intended to kill the Westerners in China and all the Chinese Christians who followed the "Western religion." However, the people respected a certain older Presbyterian missionary named Mr. Corbett. Mr. Corbett could not speak eloquently, but he had a heart to love the people. He loved everyone, and he gave whatever he had to them. Eventually, everyone came to know that this was an American who was for everyone but himself. Therefore, even the Boxers proclaimed a slogan: "Kill all the Westerners and their followers, except Mr. Corbett."

The American Presbyterian mission came to my province in China around the middle of the 1800s. The leaders of the villages gave the order that whoever saw a foreigner approaching should sound a gong for warning. All the streets would clear, the doors would close, and no one would come out. Because of this, one American missionary would hide next to a door. After several hours when the people inside would open the door to look outside, he would place a stick in the door, and then he would insert his foot. Although the people inside resisted, he was eventually able to enter. According to ancient Chinese custom, every home had a corner for grinding grain. People would mostly use mules to do the grinding, but if mules were not available, they would have to use manpower. When the missionary entered into the yard, the family would come to beat him and chase him out. However, he would find the grinding stone and begin to grind the grain for them. This changed the atmosphere. The family would go away to do other things, leaving the "foreign devil" to do the grinding. After several hours the mother would send one of the boys to take him a cup of water. It was in this way that the heart of that family was touched and the door of the gospel was opened to them. What a burden this missionary bore, and what an interest he had in people! Those who were saved through this kind of endurance were never able to forget it, and they took the same way to preach to others. This was the way that opened the doors in China.

From this account we can see what touches people's heart and what kind of burden we need to bear. Today we are not in the ancient, exclusive, conservative China. We are in America, a modern country. However, this modern country has its modern demons to keep people away from the Lord. To be sure, we need to pray for people, but there is also the need for genuine care for their souls. If we have the heart to care, we will have a way. Love can do everything; there is nothing impossible with love (1 Cor. 13:7). If we have an intensified burden and care for people, there will be a way to express this care.

HAVING A HEART OF LOVE TO CARE FOR PEOPLE

We have tried many ways to gain the increase, but little has worked. Recently, we changed from preaching the gospel in the meeting every week so that the saints could do the preaching in their homes. However, almost no saints opened their home for the gospel. This caused me to have much concern before the Lord. There is no way that works if we do not have a care for and interest in people. However, if we do have a care and interest, the care itself will open up a way. We should not say that we have no way or that no one will accept the gospel. Even the closed doors of China were eventually opened, and thousands were saved. The work in China was very difficult at the beginning. At first when one missionary went to visit the villages, no one would open the door. The children would even throw stones and mud at him. Still, he would not run away. He would stop, turn around, and say, "Thank you. That is enough." The love and endurance that this brother had for the sake of the people eventually touched their heart. The way of the gospel in every Chinese village was difficult. If we had thought that there was no need to go to places like that, then we would have had no way there.

If we had a burden, a care, and an interest for people, we could have brought in a hundred people in the last few months. Because some said that it was too difficult for the saints to bring people to the gospel meeting, we tried letting the saints preach in their homes. Eventually, however, there was no preaching in the homes. It is not that we are short of ways; it is that we are short of heart.

When the missionaries came to my province, the clans in each village would not allow anyone to rent a house to the "foreign devils." Because of this, some of the missionaries were forced to live under bridges and underpasses. In addition, no one was allowed to sell them food. It seems that they had no way to live, but the Lord had a way. One family of missionaries who lived in an underpass observed a peddler of soy bean cakes who passed by early each morning. One morning while the peddler left his cakes unattended, the missionary took a piece and put some money in its place, several times more than what the cake was worth. When the peddler returned, he found that a piece was gone but that the money had been left in its place. This went on morning after morning for a long time. Finally the peddler waited to see who was buying his cakes. He and the missionary made contact, and the peddler was saved. Under no situation should we say that there is no way. It altogether depends upon the kind of heart we have. In principle, the situation in the United States, the most modern nation on the earth, is the same today as it was in old China. The devil at that time was the ancient serpent, but today he is more modern. The same serpent uses different ways to keep people from the Lord. Therefore, we need a praying spirit and a heart to love and care for people. If we have this kind of heart and an intensified care for people, the way will be opened.

BEING RESCUED FROM
A FORMAL, LUKEWARM CONDITION BY HAVING
A GENUINE HEART OF CARE FOR OTHERS

After being in this country for over fourteen years, I have observed that many brothers are desirous for the eldership. In their consideration, the only way for them to be useful is to be an elder. They think that if they cannot be an elder, at least they must be a leader of a service group. Even the sisters desire to be leading ones among the other sisters. I have prayed concerning this situation with a great feeling of shame. In the church there should be no such ambition. We need to forget about titles and position. To be useful is not only to be in the eldership; to be useful is to pick up a burden for souls. A certain older brother who is now with the Lord was a good example to us. He was neither an elder, a co-worker, or any kind of leader, but he was used much by the Lord. He had a heart for the young people, the new ones, and new beginners. Almost every new one was invited to dinner by him. If we would all be like this, the church life will be marvelous.

The United States was built up not by its presidents but by the people, those who built up their own families in the proper way. To be sure, we need good leaders in the church life, but even more, we need every saint to be built up. Each one should say, "I love my Master, I love my wife, and I love my children. I will not go out free. I will carry out the proper service in the church. I do not care whether the meetings are high or low, living or dead, rich or poor, or hot or cold. I simply have a burden to care for at least four younger ones all year round. I love the Lord, I have a heart for the unbelievers, and I love my younger brothers and sisters."

Without being conscious of it, we have drifted into a lukewarm situation. At the present time we are drifting backward. Some have said that our meetings are too formal, but it is we ourselves who have become formal. Regardless of the way we take in the church meetings, we need to be living in our Christian life. To be the same as we were last week, last month, and even last year is the real "formality." There is no need to consider the condition of the meetings; what about our own living? A strong church can be living even without formal meetings, but it seems that now we have meetings without being living. The proper church life is twenty-five percent a matter of the meetings and seventy-five percent a matter of our living, but we have turned it around to be less than twenty-five percent a matter of our living. If we did not have the meetings, there would be no church life left.

We need the Lord's mercy. According to our numbers, we have enough saints to begin a new church in a nearby city. Because of our shortage in life, however, we dare not do this. The Lord can testify how much I have prayed. In my prayer I have thanked the Lord for all those who have been brought into His recovery. However, many dear ones who have been in the church life for a certain time are disappointed regarding their usefulness. Some even think that they cannot be useful unless they are elders or leaders in the practical service. Let us forget about the eldership and pick up a genuine heart to love the sinners and a genuine burden to take care of the younger ones. If we have a will to do this, we will surely be able. If we will all be like the older brother who had no position but always cared for the younger ones, our whole church life will be revolutionized. We must have a change. Our success depends not on our knowledge, way, or skill but on our heart. We need to pray for this and take this word for ourselves.

HAVING A CHANGE IN OUR DISPOSITION TO CARE FOR THE YOUNGER ONES IN THE CHURCH LIFE

Having a burden to care for others requires us to have a change in our disposition. Too many of us still hold on to our natural disposition. We do not contact people and invite them to our homes because they are not the same as we are. Since we are the only ones who match our disposition, we only "invite" ourselves. However, all nursing mothers are forced by their children to change their ways. A certain proverb says,

"No mother can change her children, but all the children can change the mother." However, some mothers who can be changed by their children resist being changed by others in the church life. The first time the Lord met Peter and Andrew, He told them, "Come after Me, and I will make you fishers of men" (Matt. 4:19). From that time on, their business was no longer fish; it was men. After the Lord was resurrected, He came back to Peter and said, "Simon, son of John, do you love Me more than these?...Feed My lambs" (John 21:15). The Lord made the disciples fishers of men and feeders of lambs. This is to bear a burden to care for people. In Song of Songs the Lord's seeker asked Him, "Tell me, you whom my soul loves, Where do you pasture your flock? / Where do you make it lie down at noon?" The Lord answered, "If you yourself do not know, / You fairest among women, / Go forth on the footsteps of the flock, / And pasture your young goats / By the shepherds' tents" (1:7-8). While we are seeking after the Lord, He will still remind us to follow the church and take care of the "young goats." We should not be a seeker of the Lord without any "young goats." Too many of us do not have younger ones under our care in the church life. This is a great shortcoming, and we must look to the Lord for the remedy.

No one should take the excuse that he is not gifted. Although no woman is gifted to be a mother, as a female, she is qualified to be a mother. As long as we are Christians, we all have a talent. In the parable of the talents in Matthew 25:14-30, the Lord said that there are three kinds of servants—one with five talents, one with two, and one with one. The least number of talents is one. We have at least one talent, and we need to use it. Everyone can take care of three or four younger Christians. This word is not a rebuke; it is the speaking of the truth. Since you love the Lord and His recovery, I would beg you to bring this matter to the Lord and pray for the burden. All our other concepts and dissenting thoughts are of no value. We should let the elders bear their responsibility and take the lead, and we should simply follow. What we need to do is pick up the burden to care for the younger ones, to feed the lambs in the Lord's recovery. The Lord's recovery is not the recovery of the elders; it is the recovery of all the saints. If all the saints function in this way, we do not need to worry about how good and capable the elders are.

DENYING OUR DISPOSITION AND CARING
ONLY TO BEAR A BURDEN FOR PEOPLE

According to our disposition, we like to contact people who match our taste. However, in order to invite people and care for them, we should not have a particular taste. We must receive the believers because the Lord has received them (Rom. 14:1-3). This requires us to deal much with our natural disposition. Our disposition must be touched. This is not merely a change of our behavior; this kind of change is short-lived. Rather, we need the Lord to touch our disposition. Some of us are too quick, and some of us are too slow. Some are too strict, and some are too loose. If we mean business to love the Lord and be for His recovery, we must first have a heart for the unbelievers. We should pray, "Lord, if I cannot bring one sinner to You in one year, I simply cannot go on. Lord, I am desperate. You need to give me at least one sinner." Second, we must care for the young ones, and if there are no young ones, we can still fellowship with the other saints for mutual care. In order to have this kind of heart and burden, we desperately need our disposition to be changed.

The greatest hindrance to our usefulness is our disposition. We need to let the Lord touch our disposition, and we need to deny it. Practically speaking, to deny the self is simply to deny the disposition (Matt. 16:24). We are useless and out of function mainly due to our disposition. If we deny our disposition, we will become very useful. We may be very accustomed to our disposition and have no consciousness of it. In the church life there are many kinds of dispositions. Someone may never do anything unless the elders ask him to. He may take the excuse that he does not want to act independently, but deep in his heart he actually desires the honor of being asked by the elders. This is a shame, not an honor. In the heavenly account this may be a debit instead of a credit. Romans 14:10 says that we must give an account to the Lord at the judgment seat. The Lord will ask us to show Him the credits in our account, but when we show Him something, He may say, "No, this is a debit. You did this only to gain respect and honor."

Others, however, are at the other extreme. They will do many things as long as the elders do not touch them, but as soon as the elders touch them, they will stop. They will not do something simply because the elders asked them to. They ask, "Why must I be asked by the elders? Do I not have the right to do things? Do I not have a spirit?" Everyone has his excuses. Even bank robbers claim that because the government is not fair, it is right to balance the wealth in society by robbery. With the Lord and in the church life, however, there are no excuses. Every excuse, regardless of how reasonable and fair it seems, will only cause a debit. We must be burdened for people, not caring for any excuse. Whether someone praises us or condemns us, we should have no feeling. We care only to bear people as our burden. Let others gain glory, honor, and respect. We care only for people.

Brother Nee once told us that if we do not keep the proper spiritual principles, our prayers will not be answered. The law in the spiritual realm is that we must care for people. If we do not care for people, our prayers for increase cannot be answered. If we pick up a heart to care for the unbelievers, the Lord will honor that care, and the increase will come. Likewise, if we pick up a burden to care for the other saints, the Lord will honor this care also. We all need to go to the Lord and ask Him to burden us. We should not care about our age or any position in the church. We do not even like to use the word *position* with respect to the church life. We simply need to be useful, and this usefulness is altogether in our care for people, not in doing things. To do things successfully in the affairs of the church does not mean much. The basic need in the church service is to care for people.

LEARNING TO LISTEN TO THE LORD
SO THAT WE MAY SPEAK A TIMELY WORD TO OTHERS

We have many lessons to learn. If a brother has a problem, we need to pray for him and seek the Lord for a timely word to speak to him. We need a word in season to sustain him, not gossip or vain talk. In order to have such a word, we need the tongue of the instructed, the tongue of the one dealt with by the Lord (Isa. 50:4). If we have been dealt with by the Lord, we will have a tongue that can offer a word to rescue others and sustain the weary ones. This all depends on how much we have been disciplined. Such a tongue is not that of a teacher, a professor, or a learned one but of the instructed, the taught one, the one who has been disciplined by the Lord. Only those who listen to the Lord can speak a word in season to others. This is why, in type, the slave who chose not to go out freely was brought to the doorpost so that the master could bore his ear through with an awl (Exo. 21:5-6). In order to be a good slave, our position must be at the post, listening to the master's voice. We need an opened ear, an ear that has been bored through; then we can have a proper word to speak. Even according to the physical law, one who cannot hear cannot speak well. The proper speaking comes from the proper hearing. If we do not listen to the Lord in His dealings with us, it will be difficult for us to speak a timely word to sustain the weary ones.

CHAPTER THREE

BEARING FRUIT AS BRANCHES OF THE VINE
AND
TRADING WITH OUR TALENT
AS FAITHFUL SLAVES

Scripture Reading: John 15:1-2, 6; Matt. 25:24-29; Prov. 11:25; 2 Cor. 12:15; 1 Cor. 9:22

In the foregoing chapters we saw four main points concerning our service. First, in doing things, we need life and skill. Life depends upon growth; we have the divine life within us, and this life is growing. Skill, however, depends upon training. Since the church meetings care mainly for the growth of life, we also need the training to care for our skill. Training is not for mere teaching but for dealing with ourselves without excuses. We should not be merciful to ourselves in the way of making excuses. To be trained is to become like a sacrifice on the altar. The priests showed no mercy in cutting the sacrifices. Any mercy would have spoiled the sacrifices. We need a strict training. All the ones who rendered help to me in my youth were strict. At that time I did not appreciate them very much, but today I am very grateful to them.

The second point we saw is that because the church is an organism that needs life in every aspect, merely to do business and carry out affairs in a good way is not adequate. Therefore, the church service is always for ministering life to others. Third, in order to minister life to others, we must pick up a burden to care for unbelievers, young believers, new believers, and weaker believers. If we do not contact people, we cannot minister life to them. Just as doctors need to have patients, we also need people to care for. It is impossible to minister life to others if we are always by ourselves. We need some persons to be under our care, either unbelievers under the care of the gospel for salvation or new, young, or weaker believers under our ministering of life for their growth in life. We need to pick up the burden to care for people.

Without a proper love for others, our care for them is not genuine. A proper mother cares for her children day and night. Even in her dreams, she is still caring for them. No mother would be burdened to care for her children simply because they are attractive or so that when she is old, they can take care of her. This kind of love is a political love, a love with a purpose. A mother loves her children simply because they are of her own blood. To come to someone out of a motive to accomplish something is the way of a politician. The proper way is to receive a burden for someone from the Lord in prayer and then to go to contact him, regardless of the outcome for us. After receiving a burden for some persons in a specific way, it is not effective to immediately begin to pray with them. First, we ourselves need to pray, "Lord, You have given me a burden for these brothers. Now I come to You to discharge my burden. You put the burden upon my shoulders, and now I am returning the burden to You." We need to pray through until we are assured that the Lord has answered our prayer for those brothers. We should have not merely a short, general prayer but a prayer from every angle. As we pray thoroughly, we should have the assurance that the Lord has given this burden to us and that we have returned the burden to the Lord. Then the Lord may say, "I am happy to receive this burden from your hand. Now you must stand with Me. We two—you and I, I and you—will be one. Then I will tell you the time and the right way to contact them." After this, the Lord will bring to us each one He has burdened us for. One may come the next evening, and on the following days others may come. In this way we will see that the Lord answers our prayer.

The fourth matter we have seen is that in order to minister life to others, we need to be dealt with thoroughly by the Lord. The reason we do not care for anyone is that we are too "raw"; we have not been dealt with adequately by the Lord. Almost no fallen human being was born with an interest in others. Everyone was born with an interest only in himself. However, we have been reborn, and this new birth is one that produces an interest in others. Still, we may neglect the interest that is in us by the new birth. Therefore, we need a thorough dealing, which will eventually come to the matter of our disposition. It is due to our disposition that we have no interest in others, or even if we do have an interest in others, we are unable to minister life to them. We may present people with a "loaf of bread," but within it is the "stone" of our strong disposition. If we are peculiar, it is difficult for people to receive something from us. Therefore, we must go to the Lord to be enlightened. We must not say that we have not received any light. The light is here all the time. We simply need to exercise our sight to receive it and deal with what we see. Then by dealing with what we see, we will receive more light.

THE SERVICE IN THE CHURCH
BEING IN GENUINE FELLOWSHIP
AS THE FLOW AND IMPARTING OF LIFE

As those who have been born again, we have the divine life. However, we may not exercise the divine life much in the church service. We may simply do things and talk, gossip, ask questions, and exercise our mind and emotions in the name of "fellowship," yet without the exercise of the divine life in us. To come together to have a friendly talk without the ministry of life is not fellowship; it is merely something social. Genuine fellowship is the flow and the mutual imparting of life. I minister life to you, and you return life to me, and in this life current there is the real fellowship. In our service groups if we care only for business affairs without much imparting of life, that is not the genuine church service. That is simply a kind of social service. Everything in the church must be in the nature of life, with the content of life, and in the imparting of life. The "currency" in the church "exchange" is not dollars but the divine life; the divine life is our only kind of "merchandise." The church is altogether a matter of life. Our work, speaking, fellowship, service, ministry, message, Bible study, and prayer must be in the flow and imparting of life.

BEARING FRUIT AS BRANCHES OF THE VINE

In the church we must have life, training, and fruit-bearing. Every member of the church should be a branch that bears fruit. The word of the Lord in John 15 is emphatic and definite. He said, "I am the true vine, and My Father is the husbandman. Every branch in Me that does not bear fruit, He takes it away; and every branch that bears fruit, He prunes it that it may bear more fruit" (vv. 1-2). If we are saved, we are a branch in the vine. We cannot deny this. Therefore, we must realize that every branch in the vine must abide in the Lord to bear fruit. This is not a small matter. The Lord said, "If one does not abide in Me, he is cast out as a branch and is dried up; and they gather them and cast them into the fire, and they are burned" (v. 6). Some Bible scholars have misunderstood this verse. If we take this as a word concerning salvation, we will not be able to understand it. This word is not about salvation; it is about the enjoyment of the life supply of the vine tree in order to bear fruit. To be cast out is not to be lost. Some Pentecostals use this chapter to deny that our salvation is eternal. They say that someone may be saved one day, lost the next day, and saved again the next morning. This kind of salvation can be compared to an elevator that goes up and down. However, in chapter 10 of the same Gospel the Lord Jesus said, "I give to them eternal life, and they shall by no means perish forever, and no one shall snatch them out of My hand. My Father, who has given them to Me, is greater than all, and no one can snatch them out of My Father's hand" (vv. 28-29). The Lord's salvation is eternal and once for all.

However, this does not mean that we will never suffer any dealing, discipline, or punishment from the Lord. In actuality, we may suffer all these. After someone is born, he cannot be unborn by behaving wrongly. Rather, a genuine child is disciplined when he makes mistakes. What the Lord said in John 15 is that the branches that do not bear fruit are first cut off from the supply of the vine tree, then dried up, and eventually burned in the fire. In my Christian life, I have seen many withered ones and even some who were "burned," unable to come back to the life supply. The withered ones are through with regard to the enjoyment of the life-juice of the vine tree. We must be careful not to play games with the Lord and the church. About twenty years ago, certain ones opposed, criticized, and condemned Brother Watchman Nee. Eventually, all those criticizers became withered. They did not lose their salvation, but they were finished regarding the enjoyment of the life supply.

As branches we must bear fruit. If anyone has not borne fruit for several years, I am very concerned for him. There is the danger that such a one may be cut off from the life supply. We must endeavor and be desperate. We must say, "Lord, I am one of Your branches. Why do I not bear fruit? I must bear some. I cannot go on like this anymore. Lord, have mercy on me that by Your grace I may bear at least one fruit." If we will bear even one fruit, the life supply will flood in. The life-juice will stream in, and we will bear more fruit. To bear the first fruit is a breakthrough. We must have such a breakthrough. We need to go to the Lord to have a thorough dealing with Him.

TRADING WITH OUR TALENT AS FAITHFUL SLAVES

In the parable of the talents in Matthew 25, the problem is not with the one who had five talents or the one who had two but with the one who had one talent. This one said, "Master, I knew about you, that you are a hard man, reaping where you did not sow, and gathering where you did not winnow. And I was afraid and went off and hid your talent in the earth; behold, you have what is yours" (vv. 24-25). The master did not argue with him. It is as if he said, "Yes, I am a hard man, but do not come to blame me. Since you knew who I am, you should have done the gathering and reaping." Then he said, "Take away therefore the talent from him and give it to him who has the ten talents" (v. 28). This is the divine economy. The human economy is to take care of the ones who do not have something. If someone has five talents, we would ask him to spare some for the ones who have less. However, the divine economy is not like this. The more we have, the more the Lord will add to us, but the more we do not have, the more the Lord will take from us. The reason that we do not make a profit is that we do not use the talent we have. Our excuse is that we are not apostles, elders, or leaders of a service group. However, it is good to be a "no one." The Lord does not use the "someones"; He uses the "no ones." If we think that we are someone important, we need to be reduced to be no one. When we are finally no one, the Lord will come in to use us. Therefore, we should not excuse ourselves by saying we do not know how to do something.

Too many of us are making excuses. How much profit have we made for the Lord? All the reasons for not making a profit are only excuses. We can make excuses for ourselves, but when the Lord comes, He will ask us to give an account to Him. At that time our mouth will be shut, and we will have no excuses. In this regard, the Lord is a "hard man." He admits that He reaps where He did not sow and gathers where He did not winnow. However, it is not true to say that the Lord has sown nothing. At least He has sown one talent into us. We all have something. No one can say that he never received anything from the Lord.

The Lord does not require us to make the same quantity of profit. We simply need to make a certain profit. The five talented one made five talents more, and the two talented one made two talents more. If the one talented one had made only one talent more, he would have received the same praise from the Lord. Five plus five, two plus two, and one plus one are all the same to the Lord, and He will praise each one equally. We must be careful not to fail to exercise what we have. If we are not careful, the talent we have will be taken away and given to others. The situation in the church today is not properly balanced. Some are very useful and others are not very useful, because the latter do not exercise their talent. We must all go to the Lord desperately that we may bear fruit and make some "interest" for Him.

BEING CARED FOR BY CARING FOR OTHERS

According to the divine economy of the Bible, if we desire to receive, we need to give. If we water others, we ourselves will be watered, and if we desire to grow in life, we need to help others to grow (Prov. 11:25). When we help others to grow in life, we ourselves will have the growth. The way to receive is to give, and the more we give, the more we receive (Luke 6:38; Acts 20:35). Therefore, we should not believe our situation. Our situation with respect to whether we are good or bad, useful or not useful, is a lie. We should not say that we can do nothing and are not useful. Rather, we need to say, "Satan, get away from me. I can do something, I have something, and I am useful in the Lord's hand." We should declare this to the whole universe, not by feeling or according to our situation but by faith. If we will all declare this, our whole situation will change. In contrast, the more we say that we have nothing and can do nothing, the more our usefulness is killed. The liar Satan works subtly to produce many liars (John 8:44b). Satan may use even a wife to tell her husband that he is useless, and he may use the husband to say the same thing to the wife. Satan may use even the children to say, "Don't go to the meetings so much. What use can you be to the church?" We need to speak against the lie, saying, "I do have something, and I can do something." When we say we do not have, we lose what we have, but when we say we have something, we add to what we have. Therefore, we should endeavor to water others and care for them.

Although the Lord promised a child to Abraham, the child did not come for many years. The Lord even put Abraham into a situation in which he was forced to pray for the household of Abimelech so that they could have children (Gen. 20:17). If we were Abraham, we might have found it difficult to pray. We might have said, "I am too pitiful. I have been praying for myself for many years, yet I have not received a child. How can I pray for them?" However, when Abraham prayed, God answered the prayer not only for Abimelech but also for Abraham (21:1-2). If we turn our prayer from ourselves to others, we will receive what we desire (Job 42:10). It is because we are too self-centered in our prayer that the Lord needs to teach us a lesson. If we water others, we will be watered, and if we care for others, we will be cared for.

SPENDING AND BEING UTTERLY SPENT
ON BEHALF OF OTHERS

The apostle Paul said, "But I, I will most gladly spend and

be utterly spent on behalf of your souls" (2 Cor. 12:15). This passage has the sense of sacrificing one's wealth and one's life. *Spend* refers to the spending of Paul's possessions, and *be utterly spent* is the spending of what he was, referring to his being. If we have a spirit to spend whatever we have and to be spent, to sacrifice whatever we are, we will have a great increase each year. At the present time, our rate of increase is very low. This is because we have not adequately spent what we have and what we are. We have reserved our spending and preserved our self. It is impossible to have a higher rate of increase under this condition. As we pointed out in the previous chapter, the Boxers in China had a slogan: "Kill all the Westerners and their followers, except Mr. Corbett." This is because that missionary spent everything and was spent for the Chinese people. Whenever any poor ones came to him, he would give them something, such as dinner or lodging. He reserved nothing. Eventually, when he himself was short of something, the people knew it was because he had spent it on them.

Paul was this kind of person. He always spent and was spent. He meant business with the Lord. He was on earth for nothing else but to gain people. Therefore, he also said, "To the weak I became weak that I might gain the weak. To all men I have become all things that I might by all means save some" (1 Cor. 9:22). Some in the church life are too strong in their disposition to be touchable in this way; it seems that no one can cause them to be shaped. Paul, however, seemed to have no disposition of his own. He was simply like a piece of wood that could be cut into any shape. Because his disposition was fully dealt with by the Lord, it was soft, bendable, flexible, and applicable to any situation. In my training in Taiwan in 1954, I told the serving ones that they should have a character and a disposition like paste, that can be applied to any kind of surface. On the contrary, some of the brothers and sisters are like pieces of hard rock that cannot be applied to any situation. This kind of "rock" is good only for beating others. Some may even feel good about this and say that a hard piece of rock was useful to the Lord to kill the Philistine giant (1 Sam. 17:49), but it is pitiful to think in this way. On the one hand, we need to be strong, but on the other hand, we should not be hard. We need to be soft, flexible, and applicable, good for any situation we are placed in, able to fit into every bend and corner.

DEALING WITH OUR DISPOSITION
FOR THE SAKE OF FRUITFULNESS

Our disposition is the cause for our not bearing fruit and using our talent to care for people. We are still too natural. Some persons are always slow, regardless of the situation they are in or the persons they are with. It is as if they would not even pour water on a house fire before they carefully checked what kind of water they should use. This kind of person will try to justify himself from the Bible, claiming that God is always patient and never does anything in a hurry. Brother Watchman Nee pointed out to us how the Lord once ran to do something. When the prodigal son returned home, the father ran to meet him (Luke 15:20). The Lord may be patient in every other matter, but He is quick to receive sinners. Some, though are too quick. They bear fruit quickly, but then because they offend the fruit with their quickness, eventually they have no remaining fruit. I do not care to rebuke or expose anyone. We simply must go to the Lord and let Him shine on us. Then we will see how natural we are. By His mercy, we must have a change. If we are slow, we should speed up, and if we are quick, we should slow down.

Twenty years ago I gave a training on thirty points of character. Character is different from disposition; it is thirty percent disposition by birth and seventy percent habit by our living. In order to be useful in the Lord's hand for fruit-bearing, we must deal with our disposition. In my ministry I have seen many kinds of disposition. Some people are peculiar in their way of speaking. They can make people laugh, but it is difficult for them to minister life to others. These dear ones need to be dealt with in their disposition. Some of the dear saints are too loose and light. They are never accurate in speaking or in doing things. That is also according to their natural disposition. The more our disposition is touched, the more useful we are in the ministry of speaking for the

Lord. Some were born with a disposition for speaking, but they are not genuinely useful. In order to speak for the Lord, we must be reconstituted in our being, that is, changed in our disposition. Many times I have gone to the Lord and condemned myself, saying, "Lord, I exercise my old, natural, dispositional way in speaking." Because of this, the Lord has had the ground to change my way of speaking over the years.

First Timothy 3:1 says, "If anyone aspires to the overseer-ship, he desires a good work," but to be an overseer requires that our disposition be dealt with in many directions. Other-wise, we are not qualified. We cannot be too slow or too quick, too strong or too soft. When there is the need to be strong, we must be strong, and when there is the need to be soft, we must be soft. Different situations require our disposition to be adjusted in different ways. An elder must truly be flexible. A good elder can speak a strong word of adjustment to a brother and then speak with him in a very pleasant way. However, this is not to play politics. We must be genuine. Even a small child knows whether or not someone is genuine. If someone loves a child genuinely, he knows it, but if that love is not gen-uine, he knows this also. People are able to discern. Therefore, we must not play politics; we must be what we are. The only way to be able to adjust a brother and then be pleasant with him is by having our disposition dealt with. The best way to be dealt with is to hate our disposition. Our disposition is the depth of our self, which must be denied. If we are not useful in the Lord's hand for taking care of people, it is due to our raw, natural disposition.

It is easier to deal with our disposition when we are young. Brother Nee once told us that by the time someone is fifty years old, it is difficult for his disposition and natural life to be touched by the Lord. We must not wait until we are too old to have our disposition dealt with. The earlier we deal with it, the better. Dealing with outward wrongdoings is not as important as this. The most important thing that must be dealt with in our life with the Lord is our disposition. We must learn to have our disposition dealt with by the Lord. If we pay adequate attention to the Lord and pray much about this, it will be easy for us to care for others, bear fruit, and make a profit by using our talent. Then our entire situation will be radically changed.

FRUIT BEING THE OVERFLOW OF LIFE

Many in today's Christianity teach that the reason we do not bear fruit is that we are short of power from on high. They say we should pray and fast for a certain number of days until the power comes as the baptism in the Holy Spirit. I observed this kind of practice for many years, but I still did not see much remaining fruit. For the branches of the vine tree to bear remaining fruit is not a matter of this kind of revival; it is a matter of growth. When branches receive a sufficient supply of life-juice, they bear fruit as the overflow of the inner life supply. This, not revival, is what the Lord needs. In the Gospel of John there is no hint of revival. Rather, what is revealed in this book is the genuine, growing life out of which comes fruit as the overflow. Fruit is the overflow of life. If we do not bear fruit, it is because we do not have the overflow of life; we are short and undersupplied by the inner life. For many years the Lord has restrained us from emphasizing revival. Even when we did have a revival, it was in a restricted way. What the Lord requires in His economy is the genuine growth of life. Then out of this growth, we have an overflow of life, which is fruit that remains. Brother Nee once told us that if every one-talented person in the church would use his talent, we will have a true remaining revival. What the Lord needs is not the kind of revival that comes and goes but the exercise of our talent with the growth in life. In order to have this, the basic condition is to deal with our disposition.

CHAPTER FOUR

BEARING FRUIT EACH YEAR
BY THE ENJOYMENT OF THE RICHES
OF CHRIST'S LIFE

Scripture Reading: John 15:1-2, 5-6, 16; 21:15; 2 Cor. 12:15

OUR NEED TO BE
TRAINED IN THE MATTERS OF LIFE

We need to be trained for our service and preaching of the gospel. The book of Romans covers the proper Christian life and church life. Since everything in this Epistle is a matter of life, the gifts mentioned in chapter 12 are gifts of life, not the miraculous gifts. We can illustrate the difference between life and gifts with our physical body. Eating, drinking, and breathing, for example, are not miraculous. Unless we have an extreme problem, we do not depend on miracles for the care of our physical body. Likewise, to be trained for the preaching of the gospel is not related to anything miraculous. Balaam's donkey did not need training when it received a miraculous gift to speak in a human language (Num. 22:28), but everything related to life requires training. Children need training in every aspect of their life. A small child cannot miraculously begin to speak at the age of two months. Rather, day by day and word by word, a mother trains her child to speak properly. Children must also be trained to eat properly. From birth, children have the ability to eat, but even that ability in their physical life requires some training. As Christians we are children of God. We have the divine life, and with this life there are many abilities. However, we are not superstitious to believe that as long as we have the divine life we can do everything and know everything already. Rather, we need training in every aspect of our Christian life and even the more in the proper church life.

GENUINE GOSPEL PREACHING
BEING FRUIT-BEARING AS THE OVERFLOW
OF THE RICHES OF THE INNER LIFE

The Gospels of Matthew, Mark, and Luke all speak in plain words concerning gospel preaching. Matthew 28:19 says, "Go therefore and disciple all the nations," Mark 16:15 says, "Go into all the world and proclaim the gospel," and Luke 24:47 says, "That repentance for forgiveness of sins would be proclaimed in His name to all the nations." In the Gospel of John, however, there are no such plain words concerning the preaching of the gospel. Instead, chapter 15 speaks of fruit-bearing. According to John, the Gospel of life, preaching the gospel is a matter not of mere speaking or teaching but of bearing fruit. Life is not a matter of preaching. It is a matter of growing and bearing fruit.

Although we are in the Lord's recovery, even now we are not fully recovered. To some extent we are still abnormal. Not only in our meetings but in every aspect of the Christian life and church life, we are still under the influence of old, traditional, degraded Christianity, and our gospel preaching is no exception. Deep within us is a subconscious misunderstanding and wrong influence. We consider that to preach the gospel is simply to speak a certain doctrine to people and that those who were born with eloquence can be the good, effective preachers. This is a poor concept caused by a wrong influence. Genuine gospel preaching is fruit-bearing.

In John 15 the Lord used the illustration of the vine tree to show that we, the branches of the vine, must bear fruit. If we do not understand what fruit-bearing is, we can learn of the vine tree. Branches are not good speakers, but they are good fruit-bearers. Bearing fruit does not depend upon our speaking or eloquence. It depends upon the riches of the life within us. Fruit-bearing is the overflow of the riches of the inner life. If we are short of life within, we will have nothing with which to bear fruit. Fruit-bearing is a matter not of speaking or eloquence; it is a matter of the rich flow of the inner life.

TO NOT BEAR FRUIT CAUSING US TO BE CUT OFF FROM THE ENJOYMENT OF THE LIFE OF THE VINE

Many of us do not have the sense that if we do not bring people to the Lord, we are wrong. We eat in peace and sleep in peace, imagining that we are normal. This is according to the wrong concept that we received from our background. If we lose our temper with our spouse, we immediately feel that we are wrong and are under condemnation, but if we have not borne fruit for many years, we may have no condemnation. We may feel that whether we bear fruit does not matter, as long as we are not wrong in other things. However, a branch that does not bear fruit for a long time is seriously wrong. In John 15:2 the Lord Jesus said, "Every branch in Me that does not bear fruit, He takes it away; and every branch that bears fruit, He prunes it that it may bear more fruit." The Father takes away the branches that do not bear fruit. This does not mean that the branches are lost. Being saved or lost is not the thought of John 15. Rather, this chapter shows that when we enjoy the riches of the vine tree, we bear fruit as the overflow of the inner life. Therefore, to be taken away from the vine is to be set aside from the enjoyment of the riches of the vine. This is not to be cut off from the salvation of Christ; it is to be cut off from the enjoyment of the riches of the life of Christ. This is the reason that many brothers and sisters do not have much enjoyment of the riches of Christ. They are in the church life, and they come to the meetings, but they have little enjoyment of the riches of Christ's life simply because they do not bear fruit.

The way for us to enjoy the riches of the life of Christ is to bear fruit. The more we bear fruit, the more we need the life supply and the more the life supply will come into us to meet all our needs. If you would tell me, "I do not feel that I enjoy the Lord very much," I would reply, "Go and bear fruit! Then the riches of Christ will rise up within you." Regardless of how much we seek the Lord, the spiritual principle is that if we do not bear fruit, we are cut off from the enjoyment of

Christ, the supply and riches of the vine. How much we enjoy the riches of the vine depends on how much fruit we bear. We may compare this to a water hose on a faucet. We do not wait until the water flows to turn on the faucet. Rather, as soon as we turn it on, the water comes. If the vine tree does not afford us a supply, it is because we have "turned off the faucet." To turn off the supply in this way is the Father's cutting off of the branches. The Father does not cut the branches off of the vine in order to condemn them to hell, as some teach. Again I say, John 15 is not about being saved or being lost. Instead, it shows that we are all branches of the vine with the supply of the vine. Therefore, we need to absorb the life-juice of the vine tree so that we may have the rich flow of life. However, in order to have the rich flow of life, we need to open our being, let the life flow out of us, and bear fruit.

THE NORMAL CHRISTIAN LIFE BEING
A LIFE THAT BEARS FRUIT

Many people speak of the normal Christian life, but to be normal is not only to be freed from sin according to the experience of Romans 6. This is only part of being normal. The most normal Christian life is a life that bears fruit. It is absolutely not normal for a branch on a vine to bear no fruit for many years. We must not forget that we are branches of the vine. As branches of the vine tree, we need to bear fruit.

Many of us may not care whether we bear fruit. Suppose, however, that one day a good speaker comes to us speaking in a marvelous way to stir us up. Then we will be on fire and pray constantly, praying even through the night. After a few weeks, we may be able to bring several hundred people to the Lord. However, this is abnormal. Branches on a vine are not stirred up by a good speaker and suddenly bear great clusters of grapes. Fruit produced in a miraculous way does not remain, and it may not even be genuine. We do not desire this kind of fruit. The Lord said, "I chose you, and I set you that you should go forth and bear fruit and that your fruit should remain" (John 15:16). If many people are brought to the Lord by miraculous prayer and preaching, we may proclaim that this is marvelous. However, after a short time they may be nowhere to be seen. Everyone bears children according to their own kind. Therefore, we should not blame the ones whom we bring to salvation if they do not remain as proper fruit. They do not remain because we are not proper. In order to bring forth normal fruit, we ourselves need to be normal.

If we mean business to have a proper Christian life, we must bear fruit in a normal way. This can never be done in a miraculous way. We should not expect to pray in an extraordinary way and then miraculously bring many people to the Lord. Branches bear fruit in a very normal way. When I was young, I lived near a vineyard. I saw that every year the vines brought forth only one crop. In the spring the vines began to bud, and in the fall the crop came, one crop a year. We should not dream that we can bear fruit every day or every month. Rather, we must all bear fruit in a normal way.

To bring one person to the Lord every year is normal and easy. However, in the past year many among us may not have brought one fruit to the Lord that remained in the church life. This proves that we are not normal. What then shall we do? I cannot give you a way or method to bear fruit. According to a method, we have no way, but according to life, there is a way. Therefore, not to bear fruit means that we are wrong and abnormal. We must all go to the Lord and say, "Lord, grant me to be normal in the matter of fruit-bearing. Every year I must bear some fruit. Lord, as a branch of Your vine I need a yearly crop. I do not pray for a great amount of fruit in a miraculous way. Rather, I simply want to be normal, bearing at least one fruit per year."

THE CHURCH LIFE, FRUIT-BEARING,
AND CARING FOR NEW ONES
BEING TESTS OF OUR CHRISTIAN LIFE

The test for whether a brother or sister is proper is threefold. The first test is the church life. Even if someone is considered holy and high, if he cannot go along with the church life, he is wrong. The second test is fruit-bearing. We may be in the church, go along with the church, and have no problem with the church, but if we do not bear fruit, we are also wrong. Some can pass the test of the church life, but they cannot pass the test of fruit-bearing. The third test is whether we are caring for younger believers. John 15 speaks of fruit-bearing, and John 21 speaks of feeding the lambs (v. 15). We need to take care of the little lambs. In most Christian churches, there is the shortage of the proper preaching of the gospel. In some churches, however, there is a prevailing gospel preaching, but there is still a shortage of caring for the little ones. One hundred may be saved and baptized, but only five or six remain. The rest fall away because of the shortage of the proper care. We should not complain that the leading brothers are inadequate for the need of shepherding. Rather, we must blame ourselves. If everyone among us would care for one younger one, the shepherding among us would be adequate. However, many of us regularly attend the church meetings and easily pass the test of the church, but not many pass the second test, and it is even more difficult to pass the third test. To pass only one test is to receive a grade of thirty-three percent, which is a failing grade. This is not a small matter.

FRUIT-BEARING REQUIRING US TO PAY A PRICE AND TO BE DEALT WITH

The reasons that we do not bear fruit are that we are too sloppy and slothful and that we do not like to be dealt with. If we mean business with the Lord to bear fruit, we need to pay a price. We must bear fruit at any cost. All mothers know that to bear children is not easy. Mothers have no enjoyment in pregnancy; they have only suffering. This is the price they pay to be fruitful. We may not desire to pay much of a price, but Paul said, "But I, I will most gladly spend and be utterly spent on behalf of your souls" (2 Cor. 12:15). Paul spent whatever material possessions he had, and he was spent in whatever he was in his spirit, soul, and body. If the Lord has mercy on us that we pick up the burden to bear fruit, we will immediately see that we must pay a price. If we are willing to pay the price, one of our relatives may be saved, and one of our schoolmates may be brought into the church life.

Fruit-bearing forces us not only to sacrifice but also to learn the lessons to be broken. Even if our spouse or children cannot force us to be broken, fruit-bearing will force us to be broken, if we mean business with the Lord. However, if we do not desire to be broken, we will be fruitless. Every branch of the vine that bears fruit suffers the breaking. If there is no breaking, the life-juice cannot flow out. We must not only sacrifice; we must be broken. Why have none of our relatives and in-laws been brought to the church life? Why do some of the young people not bear fruit in their school? It is simply because we are too whole. We should not say that our relatives have not been brought to the Lord because they are not good enough. We should say that it is because we are too whole. We need to be broken. Perhaps we are proud and would never humble ourselves before our in-laws. However, in order to preach the gospel in a living, prevailing way, we must be lowly, right, willing, zealous, and flexible toward people. If people are not ready to speak concerning the gospel at a certain time, we must be willing to spend ourselves to come again at another time. This is a breaking. We may prefer to choose our own time, and if we cannot choose the time, we may forget about speaking to someone. On certain days it may not be convenient to visit people, and on other days we are too busy. Then on Saturday we may need rest, and on the Lord's Day we will need more rest. We may make an excuse, saying, "I work five days a week, nine hours a day, and after working all day, I have to attend the church meetings. Then on the Lord's Day there is more than one meeting. How can I have time to contact people?" We may have a good excuse every week, but after fifty-two excused weeks the year will be lost. We must not excuse ourselves. We may have many relatives, but we may have brought none of them to the Lord simply because we excuse ourselves too much. We must not remain whole. Our entire life must be broken. If we would be broken, it will be easy for us to bear fruit. Even though we are here in the Lord's recovery, our Christian life is not normal because the increase among us is less than twenty or thirty percent. Therefore, we must pass through the test of fruit-bearing.

To care for the little lambs costs us even more. To bring forth a child is not easy, but to raise him up is even more difficult. To bring forth a child requires nine months of suffering, but to raise a child takes at least twenty years of suffering. Child-raising is very costly. Before a sister is married, she may not have any change regardless of how much others minister to her, but after she marries and has several children, these little ones become the best trainers to her. Many things that she could not and would not do, she is now able and willing to do. She becomes able to do everything for the sake of her children. For this reason I like to see all the young sisters marrying and bringing forth little "trainers." Nothing can train us as well as marriage life with little children. Even if no one else can help a sister, her little ones will train her, and she will learn the lessons. Many sisters can testify to this. The proper church life is a marriage life; therefore, we should all bear some younger ones and care for them. If we do not, we are not normal.

EVERY MEMBER BRINGING FORTH ONE FRUIT
AND CARING FOR ONE YOUNGER ONE

According to this principle, almost all of us are abnormal. We should not wait to be appointed to be elders so that we may take care of others. This does not work. In the proper church life, we do not need "pastors" or good speakers to preach the gospel and care for others. What we need is every member as a branch of the vine to bear fruit and take care of the younger ones. We should bear the burden for at least one younger brother or sister. The Lord does not require us to bear many. It is sufficient to have a yearly crop of one person as fruit and one younger one under our care. If we would all bring one person to the church life each year and care for one younger one, the church life will be wonderful. To expect a revival in a miraculous way is abnormal. We do not desire to have a miraculous yet abnormal situation. Rather, we desire to have a very normal situation in which nothing is miraculous, but everything is in life. We do not expect anyone to bring fifty people to the Lord after praying for only a few weeks. Instead, we desire that by the end of the year, at the latest, we would all bring one person solidly into the church life and be burdened to take care of one younger one. If we do this, we will learn many lessons. The church life and fruit-bearing affords us many lessons, but caring for young ones gives us even more lessons. We must all pass the tests of the church life, of fruit-bearing, and of caring for others. Our enjoyment of the riches of Christ's life and our lessons in the spiritual life and church life depend mostly upon our fruit-bearing. If we do not bear fruit, we will be cut off from the enjoyment of Christ's life, and we will forfeit the lessons in our Christian life and church life. Therefore, if we wish to constantly enjoy the riches of Christ's life and to learn the lessons, there is no other way but to bear fruit and care for others. We must bring this matter to the Lord and deal thoroughly and seriously with Him. We may say, "Lord, my eyes have been opened. Now I see that I am not normal because I do not bear fruit. I am too careless in fruit-bearing. Now I come to You to have a thorough dealing." If we would go to the Lord in this way and have a thorough dealing, the Lord will speak to us concerning a price we must pay or how we need to be broken and dealt with in certain matters. If we do not listen to His speaking, we will be cut off from the enjoyment of the vine tree, but if we do listen, we will have the deep experience of the enjoyment of the Lord's riches. The reason we are not clear concerning what to deal with and in what matters we must pay a price is that we are under a cloud, but if we listen to the Lord's speaking, our inward "sky" will be clear. There will be no need for others to tell us what to deal with; we will be clear within. We will also be clear as to which of our relatives, classmates, neighbors, and friends we should care for. The Lord will not burden us with too many.

GOING TO THE LORD TO DEAL WITH HIM
CONCERNING FRUIT-BEARING

We should not try to apply any methods when caring for others. We have learned that mere methods do not work. Even to make regulations for ourselves and to make up our mind do not work. Paul says, "To will is present with me, but to work out the good is not" (Rom. 7:18). Therefore, we should not merely use our natural will. We should simply go to the Lord and say, "Lord, I can do nothing, and I am not normal. O Lord, have mercy upon me." The Lord is the heavenly radiance.

When we go to Him, He will radiate His love and His burden into us. If nothing else forces us to go to the Lord, at least our need for fruit-bearing will cause us to go to Him. Many of us are abnormal because we have been fruitless. Therefore, we must go to the Lord to confess our fruitlessness to Him and stay in His presence and radiance for some time. Then something will be radiated into us. What we receive will be not a mere word or training from man but a heavenly "radiation." Then we will be enlightened. We will see the things that we must deal with, and we will see in what matters we must pay a price. We should not say, "Do not speak to me of paying a price. I want something for free." Rather, we must go to the Lord to deal with Him.

May the Lord impress us that we are abnormal in the matter of fruit-bearing. We must go to Him to receive a heavenly radiation. Then as we become normal, we will be the church in our locality composed of sound Christians who live a proper Christian life, not bothering people but impressing them that we in the church have something shining. This shining will spontaneously attract people and convince them. Even without our speaking to them, our relatives will be gradually convinced and attracted, and whomever we contact will be under our shining all year round. We may not speak to others about Jesus all the time, but we will have a shining, attracting power and a convincing element among our relatives, neighbors, and schoolmates. Even if they do not like us, they will have to admit that we are a higher kind of person. Then we can follow the inner "radiation" to take care of them. In this way, it will be easy to bring one person to the Lord and into the church life yearly. Eventually, everyone in our locality will know that the church is a wonderful group of people, and the church will double in size by the end of the year. At that time, every new one will be the same as we are. Just as children are the same as their parents, all the new ones will be fruit-bearing persons, and by the end of the following year the church will double again. This will build up a good reputation and credit with people. Even the unbelievers will say, "If you want to believe in Jesus, the best place to go is that church."

If we go to the Lord and remain with Him, the living Spirit will burden us to pray for certain ones among all those whom we know. To go to the street to find people is good, but this is not the best. It is better to work on people whom we know and who know us. Therefore, we need to build ourselves up among the ones we know, not in a natural way but according to Christ. Then they will all know the kind of life we live and the kind of persons we are, and they will be impressed, influenced, and convinced by us. Even if at first they do not care for us or for the gospel, they will not be able to deny that in our living there is something high, weighty, and bright. Then we can pray for them, not in a general way but in a specific way according to the inward leading. We may be burdened to pray for a certain relative for a whole month. The Lord knows how to gain that one. If we pray for him, then at a certain time he will come to us, or we will go to him. Of course, we should also have meetings for preaching the gospel, but the basic factor for the preaching of the gospel in a local church is the living of all the members. Without the daily living of all the members, the church has no ground for preaching the gospel. The gospel preaching of a local church is fully based upon the preaching daily life of all the members.

If a Christian means business with the Lord, it will be easy for him to bring one person to the Lord and into the church life. It is fair to expect this. To not do this is to go against the natural law of the life of the vine. Every fruit-bearing tree bears fruit annually. This is according to the natural law, the natural principle. The Lord does not require anything of us that is beyond the proper principle. According to the law of life, we should bear one fruit yearly. We must admit that this is true. This is the requirement according to the law of life. We should not place blame or make excuses. We must all admit that we have not lived in a normal way. If we had been normal, we would have fulfilled the requirement of fruit-bearing. From this time on, we must all go to the Lord and say, "Lord, this year I want to live a normal Christian life and a normal church life. I want to be fruitful." We must go to the Lord to deal with Him thoroughly. We should pray, not in a miraculous way but in a very normal, constant way that all

the members in all the churches will be brought into the
normal Christian life and church life with a proper preaching
and that we will all bear fruit according to the principle of
life.

CHAPTER FIVE

BEING PRUNED BY THE FATHER
TO LIVE A FRUIT-BEARING LIFE

Scripture Reading: John 15:2, 5; 1:29, 32-48; Matt. 4:13-16, 18-22

FRUIT-BEARING BEING THE NORMAL LIVING
OF THE BRANCHES OF THE VINE

Throughout the past centuries, many matters concerning the Christian life and church life were lost in the degradation of the church. Therefore, today the Lord desires to have a recovery. This recovery includes fruit-bearing. A proper Christian life is a fruit-bearing life, because we are the branches of the vine (John 15:5). God's operation in the universe is with His vine, and we are all the branches of this vine. The normal life of the branches is nothing other than to bear fruit. Whatever else a branch on a vine can do means nothing. In actuality, branches can do nothing but bear fruit. Therefore, to bear fruit is the normal living of the branches of the vine.

The important matter is not how long it takes us to bear one fruit; what is important is that we do bear fruit. To bear fruit is not merely a work, and it is not simply the preaching of the gospel. If we could ask a branch on the vine what it is doing, it would say, "I am doing nothing. I am simply enjoying the life of the vine, living, and growing, and out of this kind of living, fruit spontaneously comes forth." Fruit-bearing is not a mere work or preaching. It is a living. A living is always according to a certain life. Cats, for example, live day and night according to a cat's life. To catch mice is not their job; it is their living. Likewise, for dogs to bark is not their job; it is their living. We are branches of the vine, and our living is simply to bear fruit. Not to bear fruit means that we are abnormal, not right in our Christian life and church life.

DEALING WITH THE LORD
TO BE NEW, FRESH, AND TENDER BRANCHES

As we said in the previous chapter, the three tests of whether we are right are the church life, fruit-bearing, and caring for younger ones. If we do not bear fruit or take care of younger ones, we are wrong. John 15:2 says, "Every branch in Me that does not bear fruit, He takes it away; and every branch that bears fruit, He prunes it that it may bear more fruit." No one should say he is too old to be a fruit-bearing branch. For someone to say this indicates that he needs to be pruned. For a branch to bear fruit, it must be new, fresh, and tender. The way to be new, fresh, and tender is to be pruned. To understand the Bible in a proper way is not easy. We may think that we should wait until the Father prunes us before we bear fruit. If we wait, however, the Father may not do His work. Instead, we must all go to the Lord to deal with Him. This is the meaning of being pruned.

Our physical age means nothing. Whether we are old or new in the presence of the Lord depends upon our thorough dealing with Him. To deal with the Lord properly is not to say, "Lord, I was wrong in the past because I did not bear fruit. From now on I will endeavor and do whatever You demand me to do to bear fruit." This is a poor way to deal with the Lord; it is not a dealing but a willing. Paul says, "To will is present with me, but to work out the good is not" (Rom. 7:18). What we will to do is a work, not a living. We should not make up our mind and will to do something. Rather, we must go to the Lord to deal with Him by opening ourselves to Him. Whenever we go to the Lord in this way, we receive light. At first we may not have much light, but if we obey the light we receive and deal with what the light condemns, we will receive more light.

We must go to the Lord to have a thorough dealing with Him, opening ourselves and presenting ourselves to Him without any covering for the self. We must strip off our cover as much as possible and present ourselves fully on the altar.

We should say, "Lord, here I am. Come to enlighten me. Shine
upon me. Investigate, examine, test, and expose me. Do everything You can to bring me fully into the light that I may see
my real situation." If we do this, we will immediately see several items that we must deal with. Perhaps the first item
we need to deal with concerns our wife. We may need to
say, "Lord, forgive me. I am constantly wrong in my attitude
toward my wife." Then the Lord will demand that we go to her
to make a thorough confession and ask her forgiveness. It
seems that this has nothing to do with the preaching of the
gospel. However, we are not speaking of a mere work of gospel
preaching; we are speaking of fruit-bearing as the issue of a
proper Christian life.

After reading the previous chapter, some may go to the
Lord to say, "O Lord, forgive me. In the past I was sloppy and
abnormal. I have not preached the gospel to my in-laws, my
cousins, and my schoolmates. Lord, starting from now please
help me to contact others and care for them." As we have said,
this is not a Christian living; it is merely a willing. We should
never forget that to will is present with us, but to work out
the good is not. What we must do is go to the Lord to have a
thorough dealing with Him. If the sisters, for example, mean
business with the Lord when they go to Him in this way, He
may touch them concerning their shopping. With many of the
young people, especially the young sisters, shopping is truly a
snare, and they do not care for the Lord adequately when
they shop. In the morning they may say, "Lord, I offer myself
to You as a burnt offering to satisfy You," but afterward they
may read in the newspaper about a sale and make up their
mind to go shopping. As the tender branches, they should be
the ones who bring forth fruit. However, they have been damaged simply by their shopping apart from the Lord. Shopping
in a worldly way deadens our spirit and reduces our love for
the Lord. If we mean business with the Lord to have a thorough dealing with Him, the Lord may come first to this
matter. Then we will need to deal with it. We should say,
"O Lord, how much I need to be saved in Your life from my
shopping."

Some of the married sisters also, both in the Far East and

in America, are "addicted" to buying things. Some wives already
have dozens of pairs of shoes and several sets of silverware,
but they still like to buy more. At least, they like to window
shop. This kind of "addiction" kills the sisters' spirit. The
reason that some sisters are old, fruitless branches is that
they are old in the matter of buying things. If the sisters
mean business with the Lord to bear fruit, the Lord may say,
"Go home and get rid of all but five pairs of shoes." This is the
Father's pruning. Some sisters also love their hair, and in
these modern times, even the young men love their long hair
and beards. Some brothers may allow the Lord to touch anything but their hair. Their hair is a kind of "Holy of Holies"
to them, and their beard is a "sanctuary." In order to bear fruit,
the brothers must let the Lord prune them in the matter of
their haircut and beard. A brother may not have borne one
fruit in many years, but if he will allow the Lord to prune him
concerning his hair, he may bring someone to the Lord after
only one month. All these worldly, fleshly, and natural
desires, likes, attractions, and addictions need to be pruned.
Then we will become fresh, new, and tender.

DEALING WITH ALL THE HINDRANCES
TO HAVE A LIVING OF BEARING FRUIT

We do not need to make up our mind to endeavor to bring
someone to the Lord each year. This is not what we are saying.
Rather, we should all have a proper Christian life, a life with
no distractions, frustrations, or addictions. We should pray,
"O Lord Jesus! By Your mercy and through Your grace I am
here absolutely for You. I have no desire, likes, dislikes, addictions, or frustrations. I have nothing but You, Lord. If you give
me something, I will take it, but if You do not give it to me,
I do not desire it. I do not care for long hair or short hair.
Because I am a human, I need something to cover me, and
I do not desire to give people the impression that I am sloppy.
However, I do not love my coat and tie. Likewise, I shave every
morning because I wish to be a right person and not give
people a wrong impression, but I do not love shaving or not
shaving. I do not love anything, Lord. I love only You, and if
I love something else, prune it off." If we pray in this way, we

will be refreshed, and we will have a life that produces fruit. It is not by our endeavoring, doing, willing, or making up our mind to bring people to the Lord. That will not work, and even if it did work, we would bring forth fruit only according to what we are in ourselves. We need to be pruned by the Lord. This is a serious matter. We are not a "holiness" people, like the Amish who are allowed to wear only certain colors. We simply desire to have a proper Christian life.

More than forty years ago, when I was in Shanghai, a group of young missionaries went to China with the China Inland Mission, many of whom were sisters. Certain older sisters who had been in Shanghai for a while had learned what a Western missionary needed to do to convince the conservative Chinese people. The newer, younger sisters, however, arrived from England wearing their skirts only a little below the knee. In those days that was considered a very modern style, and some even considered it to be sinful. There was a certain older sister who loved the Lord and had been working in China for many years. She realized that all these young British missionaries with short skirts could never be fruitful. The stubborn, conservative Chinese people would say, "What is this? You are immoral. Why should we listen to you?" However, she dared not say anything to them. Instead, she served tea to them every afternoon. Then while the young sisters sat around her, enjoying their tea, she would adjust her own longer skirt. The young sisters watched her do this, and then they looked at their own bare legs. This caused them to be bothered within. Since all those young missionaries loved the Lord, they were convinced. The Lord touched them, and they dealt with Him about their dress. If they had not done this, they may not have had the peace to pray. If they had said, "Lord, save the Chinese people," the Lord might have said, "Let me save you first. Then I will answer your prayer for China." This was not simply a matter of an outward change; it was an inward touching by the Lord. In this way their preaching of the gospel to the Chinese people became a living, not merely a work.

To make our preaching a work is poor. We are not carrying out a job in our preaching; we are living a life. Therefore, if anything hinders us in our fellowship with the Lord, we should say, "Lord, prune this. I give You the freedom to cut it." This is what is meant by the Lord's word, "Every branch that bears fruit, He prunes it that it may bear more fruit." In the Lord's recovery we do not practice to have regulations. According to my own conscience, I could not smoke a cigarette and then partake of the Lord's table. However, we have never passed a regulation against smoking. We do not believe in regulations, but neither do we believe that those who smoke are able to have the best remembrance of the Lord at His table. Likewise, we cannot believe that those who love shopping can have the overflow of the inner life to bring forth fruit. Therefore, we do not wish to encourage, charge, or stir up anyone to have a mere gospel preaching work. Instead, what we need in the Lord's recovery is for many dear saints who love the Lord and mean business with Him to constantly be one with Him. We should pray, "Lord, I am one with You in my shopping. Whatever You do not want to buy, I also do not want to buy it. If You want to buy something, I will buy it only because You are buying it." We may also say, "Lord, I do not care for short hair, long hair, a beard, or no beard. I care only for You and for what You want. In my whole life, as one saved by You and under Your transformation, I like nothing and I dislike nothing. I have no love for anything else. My love is only for You. I want You to prune everything that is not Yourself." If we always remain in this condition, we will be the pruned branches.

A pruned branch always has fresh, new, tender shoots that bring forth fruit. Those who keep vineyards know that the branches of the vines bring forth fruit only at the fresh shoots. We all need to have "fresh shoots." If the sisters who love to have many pairs of shoes would say, "Lord, prune me in this matter," and they allow the Lord to do it, they will have a new "shoot" full of freshness, newness, and tenderness, and a good cluster of grapes will be brought forth. There is no need to say that we must deal with sinful matters. In the Lord's recovery we all hate anything sinful. However, there are many other items which are not sinful that we still hold on to. These matters deaden us even though we still endeavor to preach the gospel and bring people to the Lord. The Lord will not honor this kind of endeavoring very much. This is why we all need to go to the Lord, not to will or to make up our mind but to have a thorough dealing. We must lay ourselves on the altar and say, "Lord, strip off my covering, cut me, and shine upon me. Expose me, and show me the true situation with my likes and dislikes." Then if we go along with the Lord's exposing and enlightening, and we have a thorough dealing with Him, we will be fruitful.

DEALING WITH OUR NATURAL DISPOSITION TO BECOME FLEXIBLE IN CARING FOR PEOPLE

We must all be tested by the church life, by fruit-bearing, and by lamb-feeding because these are the three matters that kill our natural disposition. The church life is a killing, not of the good things but mostly of our disposition. Likewise, fruit-bearing and lamb-feeding are a killing. All these are killing "knives" for our disposition. Passing through these three tests causes us to become right, because after passing through them we become persons who have dealt with our natural disposition. Then we will be flexible. To care for little children requires much flexibility. Any mother who is not flexible should not expect to have good children. Her children will all be damaged by her inflexibility. To bear fruit among our in-laws, cousins, and schoolmates requires us to be flexible. We should not speak of inconvenience or say that we do not have time. Whether we have time depends on our desire. We may illustrate this by the need to answer correspondence. In the early years of my work, I would often apologize for not answering people sooner, telling them that I had been too busy. However, something within condemned me, saying, "It is not because you were too busy; it is because you did not have the desire." Everyone is busy. Even a sister with no husband, children, job, or school can stay busy every day. She can tell people she does not have the time for this or that. This is absolutely due to our dispositional inflexibility.

If we are not flexible, we cannot bear fruit. In order to bear fruit, we need to be flexible, available at any time, and never claiming to be too busy. We should always have time to talk to people. If we wait until we have time to help people to be saved, we may wait forever. We have all been cheated in this regard. We have said, "This week I am very busy; let me see how next week will be," but the next week we are busier and have even more things to do. Then the following week is worse, and we are never free. Being busy or available is a matter of our disposition. Therefore, we first need a thorough dealing with the Lord, and then we need to become available, flexible, and fully dealt with in our disposition.

RECOMMENDING JESUS
AS THE ATTRACTING ONE TO PEOPLE

Once we have had a thorough dealing with the Lord and have become flexible, we need something in our daily living that attracts and convinces people. The disciples mentioned in John 1 were brought to the Lord by being attracted to Him. First, John the Baptist said, "Behold, the Lamb of God, who takes away the sin of the world!" (v. 29). Later he recommended Jesus by saying, "I beheld the Spirit descending as a dove out of heaven, and He abode upon Him. And I did not know Him, but He who sent me to baptize in water, He said to me, He upon whom you see the Spirit descending and abiding upon Him, this is He who baptizes in the Holy Spirit" (vv. 32-33). Jesus is the Lamb to take away the sin of the world, and He is the One with the dove to baptize people so that they may receive God as life. These are the two attracting factors of the Lord. The Spirit of God always works through these two attracting features. Immediately after this attraction through recommendation, two of John's disciples followed Jesus (vv. 35-37). The first was Andrew, and the second should be John, the writer of this Gospel, although he was humble and did not mention himself by name. These two stayed with Jesus that day. At that time, because they were impressed, Andrew went to his brother Simon and brought him to the Lord. When He saw Simon, the Lord changed his name to Peter, which means a stone. Then three disciples were there with the Lord.

After this, the Lord Jesus went on a little farther, and He met Philip, who was of the same city as Andrew and Peter.

Then Philip found Nathanael and said to him, "We have found Him of whom Moses in the law, and the prophets, wrote, Jesus, the son of Joseph, from Nazareth" (vv. 39-45). In actuality, this is inaccurate, since Jesus was born not of Joseph but of Mary, and not in Nazareth but in Bethlehem. It was a kind of "wrong doctrine" that caused Nathanael to ask, "Can anything good be from Nazareth?" (v. 46a). Sometimes we are like Philip, giving wrong information about Christ and even about the church. However, Philip was wise not to argue. If he had argued, he no doubt would have lost Nathanael. Rather, he learned from the Lord Jesus, who had told the disciples, "Come, and you will see" (v. 39). To see is much better than to hear. Therefore, Philip told Nathanael, "Come and see" (v. 46b). Nathanael came, he saw Jesus, and he was seen by Jesus (vv. 47-48). In this way all five disciples were caught by the Lord. By this we can see that Jesus is the attracting One. Now this Jesus must be lived out in our daily life. In our daily living there should be One who is attractive and convincing. Even if we give people the wrong information, we can still learn to say, "Come and see. I have something better than a correct teaching. I have One for you to see." We need to attract people in this way.

Many of us think that if we pray and have a proper daily living, those whom we bring to the Lord will be caught right away. If we had only John 1, we may think that Peter, Andrew, and the others immediately followed the Lord. However, this is not so. If we read the New Testament carefully, we will see that the Lord Jesus went a second time purposely to catch the disciples (Matt. 4:18-22). Peter, Andrew, John, Philip, and Nathanael were all from Galilee, but Jesus' first contact with them, in John 1, took place in Bethany on the east side of the Jordan, far to the south of Galilee. In His first contact with Peter, Andrew, and John, Jesus did not call them. Rather, they all went back to Galilee to work at their jobs—Peter and Andrew to fishing and John to mending nets with his brother James. This was their old situation and old life. This indicates that even the Lord Jesus did not call people in a quick way. By this time they may have forgotten the Lord, but the Lord never forgets anyone. He knows where they are. No one came to report to the Lord, "Jesus, do You remember those men you met at Bethany? They are all fishing and mending. Go to call them!" Rather, the Lord Jesus already knew that they were there. In Matthew 4 we again see the attraction of the Lord. According to John 1, Jesus was the attracting One as the Lamb of God and the One with the dove, but Matthew 4:16 says, "The people sitting in darkness have seen a great light; and to those sitting in the region and shadow of death, to them light has risen." While walking on the seashore of Galilee, Jesus from Nazareth was a great, shining attraction. In this way Jesus went to the four brothers. His shining attracted them, and they immediately followed Him.

EXPERIENCING CHRIST AS THE ATTRACTING FACTOR TO GAIN PEOPLE IN A NORMAL WAY

Jesus' calling of the disciples was not something miraculous. We should not believe in a miraculous way. Instead, we need to have a proper living with the Lord and contact people as the Lord leads. Then people will be attracted to the Lord to a certain extent. Not everyone will be fully attracted at the first contact. Many will need another contact, and some may need many contacts. Andrew, Peter, and John were called only on their second contact, but some of the early disciples may have been caught by the Lord only after several contacts. The principle is that we should not expect people to be caught by the Lord immediately in a miraculous way. We should not care about how quickly they will be caught. We simply need to have a proper, daily Christian life and the experiences of Christ as the attracting factor. Because we have experienced Christ as the Lamb of God taking away our sins, the Baptizer with the dove, and the great light shining over us, we have Christ in His many aspects as the great attraction. This will attract people not to ourselves but to the Lord. Still, this does not mean that everyone who is attracted will be caught right away. In many cases it will take time for people to be gained.

We must all go to the Lord to have a thorough dealing concerning our Christian life and our disposition. How much we can attract people depends upon how much experience we have of Christ. Therefore, fruit-bearing should be a practical part of our Christian life. If we are all built up in this regard, we will spontaneously bear fruit each year. Whether we bear one fruit or several in one year, we will all be fruitful. The leading brothers should help the saints to be built up in this way. We all need to be built up in this kind of Christian life. We should not take the situation in Christianity as our standard; it is absolutely abnormal. Some never preach the gospel, and some preach in a foolish way, dreaming that something miraculous will happen. The proper way to bear fruit is to realize that we need a daily living as the branches of the vine, absorbing all the riches of the fatness, the life-juice, of the vine, the rich life of Christ. Then spontaneously we will have an overflow of the divine life, which will result in fruit-bearing. Every fruit will come from the overflow of the inner life. Then the church will grow not only in life but also in numbers. This is not a kind of movement or organization. It is the growth and spread of Christ as our inner life. Christ grows in us, and He spreads out from us and through us to others. This is the proper way to have fruit-bearing in the Lord's recovery.

This requires much prayer. We must all pray: "Lord, day and night grant me a proper, recovered Christian life so that I may constantly enjoy the riches of Your divine life to bring forth fruit by the overflow of Your rich life." Then we need to fellowship with one another and learn the lesson to be flexible toward others. In this way, none of our relatives, neighbors, schoolmates, colleagues, or friends will be neglected. They will all be cared for by us. Whether or not they have been predestinated is up to the Lord's mercy. We do not know this. Nevertheless, they will all be cared for by our fruit-bearing life. We will bear fruit among all the persons we know year after year. This is altogether the way the church will grow, not as a movement or so-called revival but by our proper, daily, fruit-bearing living.

CHAPTER SIX

BEARING FRUIT THROUGH
A NORMAL LIVING OF THE GOSPEL

Scripture Reading: John 4:35-38; 21:15-17; 2 Tim. 4:2

THE EXAMPLE OF THE LORD JESUS
IN PREACHING THE GOSPEL
IN A SPONTANEOUS WAY

The Revelation in the Holy Word
Being Progressive

The Gospel of John is the last of the four Gospels, and 2 Timothy is the last Epistle that Paul wrote. The last of all the books of the Bible is Revelation. Teachers and scholars of the Bible agree that the divine revelation in the holy Word is progressive, advancing from the beginning, through a process, and to a completion. In Genesis, the first book of the Bible, there are the seeds of all the spiritual matters in the Bible, but there is not the growth of the crop as the process or the harvest as the completion. It is in Revelation that we see the harvest of all the spiritual things. In the same principle, certain spiritual matters are completed only in the last of the various sets of books. For example, Matthew is not the completion of the Gospels. The completion is in John, the last Gospel. Likewise, Acts is not a book of completion. Following Acts there are all the Epistles. However, many Christians speak about the church life and Christian work mainly according to Acts. As the first book regarding the church life and Christian work, Acts has only a beginning, something in the initial stage, like a growing boy, not a mature man. If we have certain problems in our human living, it is better to go to a seventy-year-old man, not a seven-year-old boy. Only a six-year-old will go to a seven-year-old for help. Everyone always goes to someone older with more experience. This illustrates that if we have problems in the church life or in our Christian work, we need to come to the final books, such as the Gospel of John, 1 and 2 Timothy, and Revelation.

We may illustrate this principle from the writings of Paul. From the time of his earlier ministry to his later ministry, Paul's realization changed concerning certain things. First Corinthians was one of Paul's earlier books. In chapter 7 Paul expressed the wish that all men would be like he was and not marry, since marriage can be a distraction (vv. 7-8, 32-34). To those who wish to love the Lord and work for Him, wives are often a bothering, and husbands are not sympathetic. Paul wished that everyone would be like him with no entanglements. However, in 1 Timothy, one of his later books, he instructed Timothy to encourage widows under the age of sixty to be married (5:9, 14). This is because Paul had learned certain things from his further experience.

The Proper Way of Preaching
Not Being according to Traditional Christianity

Many in Christianity have a wrong impression concerning the preaching of the gospel. Pentecostals speak about preaching the gospel in a Pentecostal way, and fundamentalists speak about it in the way of revival. According to the way of revival, we first need to pray for a long time. In a training in 1951 in Manila, I pointed out to the saints that I had read that since about 1920 Christians were praying day and night for a revival. After almost thirty years, however, I had still not seen a revival. I do not trust in revivals. When I went to Indonesia a few years ago, some people told me that there had been a revival there in which the dead were raised. A certain brother who had been a missionary in Indonesia at that time witnessed this revival and entered into the inner circle of the work there. One night he saw that the leading revivalist pretended to change water into wine by exchanging the water with some wine he had prepared earlier. This deception opened the brother's eyes, and as a result, he left that work.

Speaking to Nicodemus Not about Miracles but about Regeneration in Life

In John 2:1-11 Jesus performed a genuine miracle in changing water into wine. Following this, though, verses 23 through 3:3 say, "Now when He was in Jerusalem at the Passover, during the feast, many believed into His name when they saw the signs which He did. But Jesus Himself did not entrust Himself to them, for He knew all men, and because He did not need anyone to testify concerning man, for He Himself knew what was in man. But there was a man of the Pharisees named Nicodemus, a ruler of the Jews. This one came to Him by night and said to Him, Rabbi, we know that You have come from God as a teacher, for no one can do these signs that You do unless God is with him. Jesus answered and said to him, Truly, truly, I say to you, Unless one is born anew, he cannot see the kingdom of God." Although the Lord Jesus performed many miracles, He did not commit Himself to those who were interested only in miracles. He did, however, give His time to Nicodemus. Because Nicodemus was not for miracles, Jesus could speak to him about regeneration, a matter of life. The principle is the same today. The Lord is willing to spend time even late at night to speak to only one person, not about miracles and revival but about life.

Speaking to the Woman at the Well about Drinking the Living Water

Verses 3 and 4 of chapter 4 say, "He left Judea and went away again into Galilee. And He had to pass through Samaria." Jesus had to pass this way because of one person who was chosen and predestinated by God. This example and that of Nicodemus show that it is worthwhile to spend time to talk to just one person. It was not convenient for the Lord to pass through that city in Samaria. Nevertheless, Jesus "had to pass" that way, because the Samaritan woman had been chosen by God the Father in eternity past, and it was time for the Lord Jesus to come to her. This woman believed in Jesus, not by seeing His miracles but according to the proper way of life.

Jesus was able to come to her in a wise way. If we could have been there at that time, we would have observed a thirsty Savior and a thirsty sinner. The sinner was thirsty, and so was the Savior. When the Savior asked the sinner for water, saying, "Give Me something to drink," she rebuked Him, saying, "How is it that You, being a Jew, ask for a drink from me, who am a Samaritan woman?" (vv. 7, 9). To say "give Me something to drink" does not seem like a gospel message, but one sentence later the Lord Jesus was able to turn to the gospel, saying, "If you knew the gift of God and who it is who says to you, Give Me a drink, you would have asked Him, and He would have given you living water" (v. 10). The Lord Jesus preached the gospel not in the way of traditional Christianity but in a very spontaneous way. Immediately that woman was inspired.

Since the Lord Jesus was wise, He did not preach concerning her sin. Rather, when she asked for the living water, He said to her, "Go, call your husband and come here." Because this word concerning her husband touched her conscience, she told the Lord a lie by speaking a partial truth, "I do not have a husband" (vv. 16-17a). She did not expect that this Jewish man would know all her secrets. The Lord Jesus was kind to her and did not rebuke her, but He said to her, "You have well said, I do not have a husband, for you have had five husbands, and the one you now have is not your husband; this you have said truly" (vv. 17b-18). This was truly an unveiling to her. She may have thought, "Who told this man all my secrets? He even knows how many husbands I have had and that the one I now have is not my husband."

Although she was a simple person, she was clever and turned the problem about husbands to the subject of worshipping God. It is as if she said, "To speak of husbands is not nice. Let us speak concerning spiritual things such as the right way to worship God." Nevertheless, no matter how wise and skillful we are, when we are caught by the Lord Jesus, we cannot get away. Regardless of how much we do, we are still in His hand. She said, "Our fathers worshipped in this mountain, yet you say that in Jerusalem is the place where men must worship" (v. 20). Jesus said to her, "Woman, believe Me, an hour is coming when neither in this mountain nor in Jerusalem will you worship the Father. You worship that which you do not know; we worship that which we know, for salvation is of the Jews. But an hour is coming, and it is now, when the true worshippers will worship the Father in spirit and truthfulness, for the Father also seeks such to worship Him" (vv. 21-23).

This shows that in order to drink the living water we must first make a thorough confession of our sins and then exercise our spirit to worship God. Whenever we come to the Lord, He touches our conscience concerning our past. We can cover the things in the past from the eyes of man, but we can never cover them from God's observation. Therefore, we need to confess, and if we do not confess, the Lord will confess for us. If we do not say, "Lord, I have had five husbands, and the one I now have is not my husband," He will be gracious to confess this for us. He may say, "If you are not bold and have too much shame to confess, let Me do it for you." By doing this, the Lord helped her to agree with Him, confess her sins, and repent. She may have said, "You are right. I have had five husbands, and the one I now have is not mine. This is my history, my life, and my living. What is it that I need?" What she needed was to exercise her spirit to contact God the Spirit. If she would do this, she would receive the living water.

LEARNING OF THE LORD JESUS HOW TO CONTACT PEOPLE

The Lord's way of speaking was a marvelous preaching. He performed no miracle, used no eloquence, and exercised no special skill in preaching. Rather, He spoke with her in a simple way. We must all learn to speak in this way. We do not need to attend a seminary to learn doctrinal teachings. We may simply read the Gospels and learn of the Lord Jesus how to contact people. The Lord spoke in a normal way with the abundance of life. While He spoke with that woman, He was shining over her, radiating His element into her. Because of this, she left her waterpot (v. 28). She forgot about drawing the physical water because she had received the real water. She herself became a "waterpot" to contain the living water.

She went away into the city and said to the people, "Come, see a man who told me all that I have done" (v. 29). She also performed no miracle and had no eloquence but was simply a living testimony, testifying to the people.

While she was gone, Jesus' disciples returned and urged Him to eat. The Lord responded, "I have food to eat that you do not know about" (v. 32). This means that the Savior was the living water to the thirsty sinner, and the sinner satisfied the hungry and thirsty Savior. The Samaritan woman drank of Jesus, and Jesus was fed by her. After speaking with one another, they became a mutual satisfaction to each other.

The proper gospel preaching is not a matter of revival or Pentecostal miracles. Rather, it is something normal. The Lord set up an example in John 3 by speaking at night to one man and in chapter 4 by caring for one immoral woman. This was Jesus' proper preaching of the gospel. Many today are more spiritual than the Lord Jesus was. These two chapters of John do not speak about praying, but many today tell us that we must first pray and fast for a revival to suddenly come. The Lord Jesus did not do this. It is true that Acts mentions the prayer of the church, but as we have pointed out, Acts is a book of beginnings, not of completion. John, on the contrary, is the final book among the Gospels. A final word means more than a beginning word, and in the Bible the final word is not in the first books but in the last books, such as John. According to the Gospel of John, the final word is that the Lord has no confidence in miracles. His interest is in life, regeneration, and the living water. In John 3 and 4 there are no miracles, but there are strength, power, and the riches of the inner life. We must all be impressed by the Lord as the example of the proper preaching of the gospel and not of performing miracles. In chapter 2 He performed a miracle, but He would not trust in those who were interested in miracles. After this, He immediately set forth the example of how to minister life to others by opening the door to a high-class man to be regenerated with the divine, eternal life and by helping a low-class woman to drink the living water. These are the Lord's examples for us. Today we should all take care of the gospel in such a way.

REAPING THE SEED OF THE GOSPEL
THAT HAS BEEN SOWN

The sequence of the writing in the Bible is truly meaningful. While the Samaritan woman went away to testify, Jesus' disciples came to care for His hunger. At that point, however, He began to care for them by speaking to them about reaping the harvest. He told them, "Do you not say that there are yet four months and then the harvest comes? Behold, I tell you, Lift up your eyes and look on the fields, for they are already white for harvest. He who reaps receives wages and gathers fruit unto eternal life, in order that he who sows and he who reaps may rejoice together. For in this the saying is true, One sows and another reaps. I sent you to reap that for which you have not labored; others have labored, and you have entered into their labor" (John 4:35-38). The sowing of the field of Samaria began with Moses. The Samaritans were descendants of a mixture of the Jewish people with others who had settled in that region. Around 700 B.C., the Assyrians captured Samaria and brought people from Babylon and other heathen countries to the cities of Samaria (2 Kings 17:6, 24). From that time, because the Samaritans became a people of mixed heathen and Jewish blood, they were never recognized by the Jews as being part of the Jewish people. However, history shows that the Samaritans had the Pentateuch (the five books of Moses) and worshipped God according to that part of the Old Testament. It was in this way that the seed was sown in the field of Samaria. At the least, they knew some of the things concerning God.

The Lord's word concerning worshipping God the Father in spirit and in truthfulness is difficult for many to understand. The Samaritan woman, however, had a basis to understand it. In the ancient time, the people worshipped God with sacrifices and offerings according to the law of Moses. The Samaritans went to the mountain in Samaria to worship, and the Jews went up to Jerusalem to worship. The Lord Jesus told the woman, "Woman, believe Me, an hour is coming when neither in this mountain nor in Jerusalem will you worship the Father. You worship that which you do not know; we worship that which we know, for salvation is of the Jews. But an hour is coming, and it is now, when the true worshippers will worship the Father in spirit and truthfulness, for the Father also seeks such to worship Him" (John 4:21-23). The Lord seemed to be saying, "The true worship of God is not in a place but in your spirit and not with offerings but in truthfulness. The offerings were a shadow, but I am the reality. Now you need to worship God in your spirit and with Me as the reality of all the offerings." The Lord's word indicates that the Samaritans were not heathens. They had heard a certain amount of the truth because the gospel had been preached to them in part. This means that the seed had been sown among them. This is why Jesus told His disciples that others had already sown and that now the field was ripe for harvest.

The proper preaching of the gospel is not a matter of revival or of Pentecostal miracles. It is something normal under God's sovereignty. We can apply this principle to our situation today. Almost everyone in the United States has heard the gospel to a certain extent. In this sense, we do not need to sow the seed. The seed was sown over the previous centuries. Now we need to do a normal job of going out to reap. Before the Lord Jesus passed through Samaria to gain that woman, He did not tell His disciples, "There are some persons here selected and predestinated by My Father; thus, I am going to preach the gospel. Let us go together in coordination. As I preach, you must pray." The Lord Jesus was not this "religious." The Bible simply says, "He left Judea and went away again into Galilee. And He had to pass through Samaria" (vv. 3-4). He did not announce or promote what He was doing, and He did not even ask anyone to pray. He only made a short trip, and on the way He preached. In this sense, He was not like a traditional evangelist. He simply ministered life to people, not sowing the seed but reaping the harvest. In chapter 3 He reaped one man, and in chapter 4 He reaped one woman.

TAKING THE LORD JESUS AS OUR EXAMPLE
TO LIVE THE LIFE OF THE GOSPEL

We must all be burdened to go to the Lord and be built up in this kind of life. We do not need to pray and fast for a revival. Rather, we all need to see what the proper, normal gospel is. It is that which the Lord Jesus carried out. He spent time to gain one man and spent some more time to gain one woman. He reaped not in large numbers but one by one. Moreover, He did not promote His preaching of the gospel and ask people to pray for a special activity. Rather, He simply lived the life of the gospel. Wherever He went, the gospel was His living. May we have the genuine recovery of the preaching of the gospel in the proper church life. After reading church history, I have no confidence in so-called "revivals." We should take the Lord Jesus as our example to be interested in imparting life and in helping others to be reborn and to drink the living water. This is the normal, daily preaching according to life, not according to miracles. This is what we need.

The Lord Jesus sovereignly and wisely used the illustration of a harvest to portray the proper preaching of the gospel. A harvest cannot be prepared overnight. A harvest comes about through tilling the ground, sowing, watering, and caring for the crop for a certain amount of time. First, the ground should be tilled and the seed sown. After this, it should be watered and cared for, and finally the harvest will come. This is a matter not of miracles but of a process in life. It is not right to expect a great revival that suddenly brings in a thousand people. We should awake from this kind of dream, realize what the proper gospel life is, and live it out in the church. Wherever we are, the gospel is with us, because it is our life. Without the living of the gospel, the church life is empty. We must all learn the example of the Lord Jesus.

PROCLAIMING THE WORD,
BEING READY IN SEASON AND OUT OF SEASON

Paul told Timothy, "Proclaim the word; be ready in season and out of season; convict, rebuke, exhort with all long-suffering and teaching" (2 Tim. 4:2). We should not say that it is winter and that we need to wait for spring to sow the seed. Rather, we are peculiar farmers; to us every day is for sowing the seed and for reaping the harvest. "In season" is when we have the opportunity, and "out of season" is when we do not have an opportunity. Whether or not we have the opportunity, we need to be ready. To "be ready" means being urgent, attentive, and on the alert. We can compare this kind of readiness to instant tea or coffee. Whenever we need some tea or coffee, it can be ready instantly. We need to be "instant" preachers, ready without need of further preparation. We should be ready at any time and in any place. We are ready at the supermarket, the bus station, the office, and the classroom. We must not say that we are not ready or that there are no opportunities. Every occasion—spring, summer, fall, and winter—is the time for us to be ready. This is not the religious way of preaching. This is the proper Christian living. There is no other way to take. We need to have this kind of gospel living. We should not say that this is not the right place, the right time, or the right person for the gospel. Every place is the right place, every time is the right time, and every person is the right person. We must be instant, ready, urgent, and attentive in season and out of season.

NOT EXPECTING A GREAT REVIVAL
BUT BEARING FRUIT IN A NORMAL WAY

In the two Epistles to Timothy there are no miracles. If we have miracles, then we do not need to be in season and out of season. We can simply pray for three nights, and something will come down from heaven. However, the gospel is not that way. Many Christians have prayed in a superstitious way, expecting a great revival to come, but the result has been poor. If, on the contrary, Christians will have a normal living of the gospel, it will be sufficient for each one to bring only one person to the Lord each year. Then within twenty-five years the whole world will be evangelized. Even in our own locality, if we all bear one fruit in a year, our numbers will double until the whole city will be evangelized. This is much greater than the biggest revival.

The subtlety of the enemy causes us to be too farsighted, looking to the future while neglecting the present. We do not need to look to tomorrow, and there is no need to pray for three years for a great revival to come. We should simply live for today and take care of one "Nicodemus." Many of us have been in Christianity for many years, and until today we are still under the influence of its traditional concepts, understanding, and teaching. We must be rid of all these concepts. We should care only for today, not for tomorrow. Perhaps this evening we will meet one of our relatives. Then we should spend some time to take care of him. This is a normal, daily gospel living, not a movement or special activity. The Lord Jesus went to Samaria in a very normal way and waited at Jacob's well for someone to draw water. Then He asked her for water, not in the way of preaching or of a movement but as part of His normal daily living. This daily living was His gospel preaching. Because He was living in this way, God sent the right people to Him, and He brought people to God. If we would all live in this way, God will send His chosen ones to us. Then every year we will reap fruit. However, because we have been influenced by the wrong concept, we have not borne fruit in a normal way. Our time has been wasted in vain expectations, and we have not lived out our duty. If we have the proper living, day by day and one by one people will be brought to the Lord and into the church life. This is the proper preaching of the gospel.

FEEDING THE LORD'S LAMBS
ACCORDING TO THE NORMAL PROCESS OF LIFE

John 4 speaks concerning reaping the harvest, John 15 concerning bearing fruit, and John 21 concerning feeding the lambs (vv. 15-17). No one can feed a lamb once for all in a miraculous way. If we try to do this, we will kill the lambs. Rather, we need to feed them daily, several times a day, just as mothers feed their children meal after meal. We need to turn from the miraculous concept to the life concept. The Gospel of John is a book on life. Reaping a harvest, bearing fruit, and feeding lambs are all processes of life. These are all related to a daily living in the way of life, not a mere work, activity, or movement in a miraculous, religious way. If we receive the Lord's mercy and enjoy His grace, we will all be built up in this life, and we will bear fruit and even double each year in a normal way. Then in less than ten years the entire city we live in can be converted. This instant and constant way is solid, rich, and prevailing. This must be our living day and night.

By living this way and being such persons, we will constantly enjoy the Lord's presence, supply, and all the riches of the life of Christ. We will have much to minister to the saints and much with which to function. This will enrich and uplift our meetings, and it will make us living and joyful.

A family that has only the older generation with no children is not a joyful one. There is no doubt that to care for children is a bother. Because my grandchildren are much trouble, they can stay with me for only short periods of time. Nevertheless, I love them all. How poor it would be if at my age I had no children or grandchildren! My highest joy, however, is all the dear saints. We are a big family with all ages. Even a few new ones added to the church will make the meetings new, fresh, uplifted, and enriched. If the "older generation" of saints were the only ones who met all year round, we will all be disappointed, but if every Lord's Day we have several new ones, our spirit will be uplifted. To bear fruit in this way is the normal living of the church life. We must all be built up in the living of the gospel.

CHAPTER SEVEN

SERVING IN ONENESS AS THE HOLY AND ROYAL PRIESTHOOD TO BE BUILT UP AS A SPIRITUAL HOUSE

Scripture Reading: 1 Pet. 2:2-5, 9; John 1:51; Gen. 28:11-22; Psa. 133

THE PRIESTHOOD BEING A BUILT-UP SPIRITUAL HOUSE

It is not easy for Christians to understand what the real service is that we render to the Lord. The natural thought is that anything we do for the Lord is a service. The word *service* has even been damaged in Christianity today. People speak of the Lord's Day morning meeting as a "service," and in the evening they also have an "evening service." What they mean by *service* is simply a Christian gathering. In the Bible, however, service has a much different meaning. The best portion to see the proper understanding of the service is in 1 Peter 2. Verse 5 says, "You yourselves also, as living stones, are being built up as a spiritual house into a holy priesthood." In the original Greek of the New Testament, there are two words translated as "priesthood" in English. One word is used in Hebrews 7, referring to the priestly service, the service of the priests (vv. 11, 12, 24). The other, used in 1 Peter 2:5 and 9, refers not to the priestly service but to the group of priests, the priestly body. The spiritual house in verse 5 is the priesthood, the priestly body, and this priesthood is the spiritual house. Both the spiritual house and the holy priesthood are being built up. Verse 5 continues, "To offer up spiritual sacrifices acceptable to God through Jesus Christ." To offer is to serve; the offering up of spiritual sacrifices is the real service. The true service which we render to the Lord is an offering by a built-up body of priests, and this built-up body is the spiritual house. By this we can see that the genuine, proper service depends upon the building. If there is no building, there can be no house, and if there is no house, there can be no priesthood. The building is the house, and the house is the priesthood, the priestly body.

Today we speak of "service groups" in the church. This is a good term. In the biblical language, the service groups are the priesthood. "Service group" is simply a modern way to refer to the classical, or scriptural, term *priesthood*. The service of arranging chairs is a chair-arranging priesthood, and the cleaning service group is a cleaning priesthood. We also have the junior high, nursery, and clerical priesthood. The word *priesthood* should remind us that our service groups are the building up of the priests. If we are not serving as priests in this way, what we have is not a service group. Those who arrange the chairs in the meeting hall are not merely chair arrangers; they are priests. This means that they not only arrange the chairs; they render a service to God. Chair arranging is not their business, duty, or service. Their service is something holy and spiritual. In itself, chair arranging is not holy or spiritual; it is not a service. Our chair arranging is different. It is a holy and spiritual service rendered to God.

The first test of our service is whether we are serving as priests. The second test is whether we are serving as individual priests or as the "hood," the corporate priesthood. Those who arrange the chairs are priests, but this is not enough. They should serve not as individual priests but as the priesthood. Priests are many, but the priesthood is one and unique. In the service groups there is only one priesthood, which is composed of the many priests. This implies the building up. The genuine service in the church has the nature of being priestly and of being built up. If our service is not of this nature, it is not genuine; it is a counterfeit and an imitation. Our service is a priesthood.

THE PRIESTHOOD BEING HOLY AND ROYAL

A priest is not a common, natural person. Of the billions of people on the earth today, relatively few are priests. They are merely common people. A priest is, first of all, one who is separated, not common. Everyone in the church service must be a separated, sanctified, marked-out person. This is why 1 Peter 2 says that the priesthood is holy. It is something special, separated, and sanctified. We must not be common in our thinking, attitude, speaking, expression, in the way we dress, and in every matter and every aspect of our living. If we are common even in one matter, we will lose our standing as priests. A priest is a holy, separated person. In the ancient time among the Israelites, the priests clothed themselves, ate, and lived in a different way, and they lodged in a different building. This was a type, but today the reality is the same in principle. As priests we must take care of what we are. We must be separated, different, and not common. We must be special. Some may say that we need to be "human," but we need to be careful when we say this. If we are "human" in a common way, we are finished as priests. We need to be human in a holy way with a holy humanity. This is the meaning of being a priest.

Moreover, a priest must also be royal, or kingly. First Peter 2 speaks of both the holy priesthood (v. 5) and the royal priesthood (v. 9). To be royal is not only to be uncommon and special but to have a high standard. Many dear saints love the Lord and know the church, but the way they behave, speak, and do things is too low, not like kings. We must not be proud, which is to be ugly and foolish, but we should not forget that we are kings. We are high persons who belong to the royal family. This also is included in the matter of service. Those who arrange chairs are royal chair arrangers; they are kings arranging the chairs. In this way, chair arranging becomes a kingly service.

Some Christians are ambitious for position in the church. They desire to be one of the leaders, even the leading one among the leaders. We should not care for whether we are elders, leading ones, or simply small brothers with no name. Rather, we should care for the kind of person we are. If a beggar ascends to a king's throne, his kingship will be beggarly, but if a king sweeps the street, his street sweeping will be kingly. If the chair arranging brothers and sisters are kingly, the chair arranging in the church service will be kingly, and people will see something high. They will not see a group of lowly workers arranging the chairs; if this is all that people see, we are altogether a failure in our church service. Instead, the new ones should be able to see something high and kingly even in the lowly affairs such as chair arranging and cleaning the hall. Whether these matters are high or low depends on who does them. If the President of the United States comes to arrange the chairs, the chair arranging would be a great matter. Arranging chairs is the same business one way or another. What makes a difference is who does it. We are the holy and royal priests. We must be holy, separated, and not common, and we must also be kingly, with a high standard. In the church service even the young ones should consider themselves kingly.

IN OUR CHURCH SERVICE, PAYING OUR FULL ATTENTION TO THE PRIESTHOOD AND THE BUILDING

We all need to be built up as the Body, the priesthood, and the spiritual house. The building as God's goal is a crucial, significant, clear, and definite matter in the Bible, yet for almost two thousand years the Lord has not fully accomplished His purpose and attained His goal. Among the many teachings, messages, and sermons in Christianity, almost none of them ever speaks of God's building. I learned from the teachers in the Brethren assemblies that Christ is the living stone, and we come to Him as living stones, but these teachers did not mention that the stones are for the building. To hide the New Testament teaching of the building is the subtlety of the enemy. Today the Lord's ministry cannot neglect the matter of the building. Even in coming to the Gospel of John, we must see the building of God. John speaks concerning life and building. In John 1, John the Baptist recommended Christ as the Lamb to take away sin and as the One with the dove to bring God as life (vv. 29, 32-33). This attracted five disciples, among whom was Simon, whose name the Lord changed to Peter, meaning a stone (vv. 41-42). Later when Jesus met Nathanael, He said, "Behold, truly an

Israelite, in whom there is no guile!" (v. 47). When Nathaniel asked how Jesus knew him, the Lord replied, "You shall see heaven opened and the angels of God ascending and descending on the Son of Man" (vv. 48-51).

The Jews at that time would have realized that Jesus was referring to Jacob's dream in Genesis 28:11-22. In this dream, Jacob saw a ladder set up on the earth, whose top reached to heaven. When he awoke, Jacob poured oil upon the stone on which he had slept, and he called the name of that place Bethel, which means "the house of God." In mentioning this to Nathanael, the Lord's intention was to indicate that as the Son of Man He is the ladder that keeps heaven open to earth and joins earth to heaven for the building of the house of God, Bethel. John 1 begins by saying, "In the beginning was the Word, and the Word was with God, and the Word was God...In Him was life" (vv. 1, 4a), and it concludes with the house of God. Thus, in John we have life and building. By all this, Peter received a deep impression. No doubt, he could never forget how his name was changed to "stone." In eternity we will remember that Peter is "stone," and he will remind us all that we too are stones. Therefore, when he wrote his first Epistle, he said that the Lord Jesus is the living stone, and we all are living stones coming to Him to be built up as a spiritual house.

We must keep the building of God as our standard. For almost two thousand years the Lord has not gained His building among the believers. Because of this, Satan can challenge Him and say, "Did You not say in Matthew 16:18 that You would build Your church and that the gates of Hades could not prevail against it? Where then is the builded church? I have prevailed to frustrate the building." It is a shame to the Lord if we do not have the building among us. Therefore, in our church service we must pay our full attention to the priesthood and the building. We must be the priests, and as the priests we must be built up together. If as thousands of persons we are built up as one man, this will be a shame to the enemy. It is against this built-up church that the gates of Hades cannot prevail.

If we mean business to have a proper service group, we should go to the Lord to check whether or not we are priests, separated persons, holy and royal with a high standard. We are still on this earth, and most of us have a job in the secular world, teaching or working in an office. However, we must be holy and royal in order to tell out the virtues of the One who has called us out of darkness into His marvelous light (1 Pet. 2:9). To tell out is to proclaim abroad, to declare, the virtues of Christ. If we are not holy and royal, we cannot proclaim abroad the virtues of Christ. We are not the proper priests; rather, we are merely common persons on the earth. In this case, what we do is not a service; it is only a kind of job or business. If we desire what we do in the church to be a service, we must first be priests. Then we must not serve in a separate way. We must be one with others.

DEALING WITH THE SELF
AS THE SOURCE OF DISSENTING OPINIONS
THAT UNDERMINE THE BUILDING UP OF THE BODY

If we are not built up, the gates of Hades will prevail against us. If even at this present time there is a lack of building, the enemy will prevail. This is why Satan is subtle to undermine the building through dissent and opinions. When I hear certain dear ones say, "There is no doubt that the Lord is blessing this church," I am prepared for them to continue by saying, "but..." Then they will itemize all their dissenting opinions. They may say that the elders, the brothers, the sisters, and all the children are not good. The subtle enemy is very clever. He will often point out things that are true. However, something that is true may cheat us the most. The enemy uses these things to undermine the building, and when this happens, he is able to prevail against us.

To be a holy and royal priest is to be fully separated from the world, and to be built up together is to be fully out of our self. Therefore, we must deal with the world, and we must deal with our self. The self includes our disposition, thinking, and ways. If we mean business with the Lord to be in the church service, both the world and our self must go. There is no world and no self in the service. Any element of the world will cause us not to be the priests. In order to be priests, everything worldly must be cleared up. Likewise, in order to be built up, we need to be saved out of our self. The self must go, including our disposition, our likes and dislikes, our way of thinking, and our way of doing things.

We must learn not to be dissenting, but simply not to be dissenting is insufficient. The root of dissent is the self, our disposition. There is always something to criticize about others. Someone may say, "I like this brother. He is a dear saint, but he is a little sloppy. Look at the way he dresses and the way he speaks." Even the Lord Jesus often suffered people's criticism. If we were as perfect as the Lord Jesus was, we would still be criticized. Some who are in the service groups may subconsciously hold a criticizing concept, saying, "The church is good, but..." This is according to the fallen disposition. We all are human, and we all have a disposition. Only something that is not living has no disposition. However, our disposition has been poisoned by the old, cunning, subtle serpent. Whenever we say, "But..." in a criticizing way, that is the subtle serpent. We do not mean that the church is perfect or that everything among us is excellent. It is simply that if we are built up together, we will not speak this kind of criticizing or dissenting word.

We may be positive about the church at first, but soon afterward one of the elders may offend us, or we may be offended when we do not receive something we expected to receive. Then if we become negative, everything is wrong. Even the way the chairs are arranged is wrong. We may ask, "Why are the chairs in a square? Why are they not in a circle?" However, even if next time the chairs are arranged in a circle, we may say that the circle is too small or that the seats are too far apart. There will always be something to criticize. This happens simply because we lack the building up. The building does not depend upon things being perfect. Until we are fully glorified, there will always be shortages. As long as we are still in the old creation, we cannot expect everything to be right. We cannot expect the leading ones to be perfect. Neither they nor anyone else has been perfected as precious stones. We are still under the process. We should all be "butterflies," but we are only halfway out of the cocoon. No one is perfect yet.

KEEPING THE ONENESS FOR THE BUILDING UP
OF THE BODY BY NOT CRITICIZING OR DISSENTING

The New Testament tells us that there are a few things that we must not tolerate. If anyone worships idols, we should cleanse ourselves of him, and if a brother is in immorality, we must ask him to repent (1 Cor. 5:11; 2 Tim. 2:20-21). To ask a brother to repent is not a criticizing; it is a loving admonition. Likewise, we cannot tolerate division, and we will not receive anyone who denies that Jesus is the Son of God or claims that the Bible is not divinely inspired (Rom. 16:17; Titus 3:10; 1 John 4:2-3; 2 John 7, 10; 2 Tim. 3:16). As to other matters, however, it is better to care for the building up by not speaking a word of criticism. Criticism always comes from a dissenting disposition, and it undermines the building. Whether a brother cuts his hair long or short or whether he has a beard or shaves, we should not say anything. Likewise, whether the sisters wear short skirts or long skirts, we should not speak a word. These matters are up to the Lord's grace. If someone arranges his home in a nice way or a messy way, we should simply let that go. We must stay away from any kind of criticism, because criticism comes from dissension, which has its source in the fallen disposition, in which Satan, the subtle one, is lodging. This damages the building. Instead, we need to preserve the building.

When we come together in the service groups, we must first keep the oneness. If the leading brothers in the service ask us to arrange the chairs in a peculiar way, we should not speak a dissenting word. We should simply do as they say. Even if arranging the chairs in that way seems foolish, to go along with the brothers is much better than to be dissenting. There is no need to argue with them to show that we know more than they do. To do that would truly be foolish. Since those brothers are taking the lead, we should do as they say. Perhaps after a further time of prayer they will ask us to arrange the chairs in a more appropriate way. In that case, we should not be offended. We can simply say, "Praise the Lord for His wisdom" and do as they ask. Although this is an extreme example, it illustrates the need of oneness in the church life. If there is a situation of oneness among us, people will be impressed. They will say, "Surely this is the church life." However, we may argue with the brothers and say, "You are foolish. How can we set up the chairs in this way?" In this case, people will say, "This is not the church. It is a place of fighting." What matters is not the way we do things; what matters is the oneness.

After being in Southern California for over twelve years, the brothers here can testify that I have not dissented from them. Whatever they say, I go along. Some have said that the brothers here only say yes to me. In actuality, it is more often the case that I say yes to them. Quite often they ask me how I feel about something but go on to do it differently from my feeling. I am never unhappy with them. I simply say, "Praise the Lord. Your way is better." This is the way I served with Brother Watchman Nee in China. After a revival was brought in to the church in Hong Kong through Brother Nee, he cabled me to come and arrange the service of the elders, deacons, and the whole church there. One night after I arrived, he turned the meeting over to me. I told him, "Brother Nee, as long as you are here, I will follow you and not speak anything of my own." This demonstrates that in the Lord's work in the church, the first matter is the oneness.

LEARNING TO GO ALONG WITH OTHERS FOR THE SAKE OF THE BUILDING UP

We should not think that we are smart and have a better way. Even if our way is better, we should not make a show of it. If the Lord puts us in the position of "driving the car," then we should drive it, but if He makes someone else the driver, we should let him drive. No one wants a back-seat driver. I have watched brothers fight about the way to drive somewhere. A ride may take twenty-five minutes, but a smart brother may know a shortcut that saves ten minutes. However, if he fights with the driver about taking the shortcut, the whole ride may take an hour. The driver will insist that he is in control, and the passenger will tell him to humble himself and listen to others. This is foolish. This kind of fighting exhausts the brothers, upsets them, and stirs up their mind. The wise way is to let the driver do his job. The difference between the long way and the shortcut means nothing, but the fighting means very much. We should never fight. If the driver takes the long way, we should praise the Lord and use the extra ten minutes to rest. We must never argue or dissent. Whatever the brothers do, we should simply go along.

Many times I agreed with the leading ones in the church here simply to be one with them. We cannot expect that everyone will be like us. If I expect all the saints in all the churches to whom I minister the word of the Lord to be the same as me, I am the most foolish person. The wisest way is not to expect others to be like ourselves. A husband cannot even expect his wife to be the same as he is. She is a female, and he is a male; how can she be the same? Because they are two different persons, it is impossible to be exactly alike. Therefore, the restful, happy way is to go along with others. A husband may not like to eat something, but the wife will say it is healthy for him. In that case he should praise the Lord, not complain, and simply eat it. We must learn to go along with the dear saints. As long as they are not in idolatry, immorality, division, or blasphemy to the Lord Jesus, we should go along with them in every aspect. What they are doing is not wrong. Whether they desire to read Genesis or Revelation does not matter. Every book of the Bible, even every page, is wonderful. There is no need to argue. To read one book rather than another may be good, but to dissent is poor. We must learn not to be dissenting.

Psalm 133 says, "Behold, how good and how pleasant it is / For brothers to dwell in unity! /...For there Jehovah commanded the blessing: / Life forever" (vv. 1, 3b). We must believe this short word. The Lord commands His blessing of life where the oneness is. The blessing is not on our being right; it is on our being one. To keep the oneness is not to keep being right. Being right has no clear standard. Our sight in this matter is not trustworthy. Ten years ago a certain tie may have been considered too wide, but today it is too narrow. There is no definite standard as to how wide is wide and how narrow is narrow. Therefore, we should not think that we are right. I say again, there are only a few things that we cannot receive: idolatry, immorality, division, blasphemy, and not believing in the divine Word. Otherwise, whatever the saints do is all right.

No one can have the assurance that his way is right. How can we say what the right way is to arrange the chairs? Right or wrong depends upon our view, understanding, purpose, vision, and background. Therefore, we must not dissent or contradict. We should simply praise the Lord and be one with the dear saints. Because we are in the Lord's church, His Body, and the way of His recovery, we have no opinion. We are on the way to reach the goal. We may get there in two days, two months, or two years, but Hallelujah, we are on the way! Only the Lord knows when we will reach the goal. If someone insists that his way is the short way to a destination, it will eventually be the long way, because there will be fighting the whole time. We have seen this in the history of Christianity, and we should not repeat it. The oneness is precious; may the Lord Jesus help us to keep it.

We must all be built up as a spiritual house, which is the holy and royal priesthood to offer up spiritual sacrifices. As long as we are built up in this way, whatever we render to the Lord will be an offering. This is our service to Him, and it will show forth the virtues of Him who has called us. No one can say which way is right or wrong. The only right way is the way of building. As long as we are one, we are right, but if we are not one, regardless of how right we feel that we are, we are wrong. The only right way is to keep the oneness.

PRACTICAL APPLICATIONS
IN OUR CHURCH LIFE AND SERVICE

Not Making Demands on Others
or Judging Them Superficially, but Knowing Them
according to Their Deeper Condition

We often expect that others will change according to our concept and standard. Rather, we should always go along with others; then there will be no problems. If two brothers live together, one may like to rise early, but the other may rise up later. In this case, the one who rises earlier should sacrifice his way. Then one day the second brother may begin to rise even earlier than the first one. This illustrates that to contend about the right way is not necessary. On the day of resurrection two disciples were going down to Emmaus. When the Lord Jesus joined them, He did not say, "You are going the wrong way. This bothers Me, and I cannot go along with you unless you turn around. Since you are My disciples, you should go along with Me." In terms of right or wrong, those two disciples were wrong. However, the Lord Jesus did not say anything about it. Instead, as they were going down, He went down also (Luke 24:13-15). Then He acted as one who did not know anything, asking, "What are these words which you are exchanging with one another while you are walking?" (v. 17). One rebuked the Lord Jesus, saying, "Do You alone dwell as a stranger in Jerusalem and not know the things which have taken place in it in these days?" (v. 18). To be sure, Jesus knew much better than they did. If we were the Lord Jesus, we might have said, "Do you not know who I am? I am that person whom you are talking about." Instead, the Lord Jesus simply went along with them to a certain place, and when they arrived, they stopped to eat. The Bible does not tell us how, but at that time their eyes were opened, and they recognized Him. Then the Lord disappeared, and the disciples rose up and returned to Jerusalem (vv. 28-33).

This account of the Lord Jesus in Luke 24 illustrates that we should not make demands on others. The brother who likes to rise early should simply go along with the one who sleeps longer. If the first brother is not already a sloppy person, then sleeping longer for the sake of the other brother will not make him sloppy. Instead, his sleeping later will be for a proper reason. Then there will be no arguing between the brothers. Shallow persons see things only according to their appearance and endlessly fight over them. We should not see things in a shallow, childish way and consider whether someone is right or wrong. Perhaps we are wrong, and perhaps someone else's way is better than ours. We should be patient for a while and wait to see the real situation. To criticize people is to judge them, but who are we to judge? How do we know that we are right and others are wrong? To judge quickly is superficial, and to say absolutely yes or no is childish. What is right or wrong does not depend upon what is on the surface; it depends upon what is deeper. We must learn to know people according to their deeper condition. If we do this, then by the Lord's grace there will be no problems among us.

Not Having a Definite Way in the Service but Going On by Prayer and Fellowship

In the church service we do not always need a definite decision about matters. In many matters we may not know what the right decision is. In almost all the Lord's work concerning the church affairs, we are like Abraham. When he was called, he went out, not knowing where he was going (Heb. 11:8). He did not have a definite decision. Rather, what he had was the Lord's presence step by step. If we go on step by step without a definite decision but with a praying spirit and a spirit of depending one upon another, the Lord will lead us. This is the best way to go. It is not good always to have a definite way in our service. It is better not to have a way. Then we will pray more, seek the Lord, depend on the Lord, and fellowship with one another.

Not Insisting That Others Remain Where They Are Assigned in the Service

If someone feels that it is better to serve in a different area than where he is first assigned, it is better to let him make the change. After he makes this move, he will better appreciate where he should be. No one should have too strong an assurance that his feeling is right. Perhaps to move to another service group is right. Only the Lord knows, and even if we do know, we should still not insist that we are right. Eventually, the brother will learn the proper lesson, and if he was wrong, he will come back. It is better to be spontaneous and not insist on anything. Then we will not cause problems. If we insist that the brother remain where he was assigned in order to learn a lesson, it may be we who need to learn a lesson. We should never insist in this way.

Not Participating in Any Negative Talk

We should never participate in criticism, complaining, or arguing. To receive such negative talk is to be a "trash can." If others criticize or speak in this way, we should excuse ourselves in a nice way. The more we allow ourselves to be involved with complaining, arguing, or vindicating, the more we are contaminated and receive the poison of death. We should stay away from this kind of talk. Then the next time people come to us, they will come without this kind of criticism. They will simply come to fellowship and pray. This is the proper way to shepherd one another.

Not Making Proposals, but Accepting Others' Proposals in Order for Everyone to Learn the Lessons

Our basic need is to learn how to be the priests built up in oneness. The way we do this depends on our spirit. We must have a spirit of not dissenting and not showing that we are smarter than others. Then we must also try not to propose other ways to do things. To propose other ways always sets up a bad example for others. In the church life, the best way is not to propose anything. If the "steering wheel" is under our hand, others should listen to us, but if it is in someone else's hand, we should not try to drive.

If someone genuinely asks us for a proposal and he truly needs it, and if to make a proposal does not set up an example of dissension, it may be the right time to do something. Whether or not to propose something depends on the situation and on our spirit. However, if someone else is taking the lead, we should listen to him. In this case, even if our proposal is better than his, it is better not to say anything in order to keep the standard of oneness. As long as we keep the oneness, we will save much time and be saved from many things, but if we lose the oneness, we will suffer loss in many ways. We may gain something in one way, but we will lose in many other ways. In general, therefore, it is better not to propose anything. Then we will gain and not lose. Still, if someone does propose something, we should go along with it. In this way everyone will learn. If we never do what someone proposes, he may not learn the lessons, and we ourselves may not learn anything either. When the real nature of the proposal comes out, everyone will learn something.

CHAPTER EIGHT

PRACTICAL POINTS
CONCERNING SHEPHERDING

Scripture Reading: 1 Thes. 2:7, 11; 2 Cor. 12:15; 1 Cor. 4:14-15

A FURTHER WORD CONCERNING THE BUILDING UP
OF THE BODY OF CHRIST

To Be Built Up Requiring Us to Deal
with Our Peculiarities

As we saw in the previous chapter, the main thing we need in the church service is the building up. Because most Christians do not realize the need for building, Christianity today is mainly a group of organizations. A building is not merely a collection of materials. The true nature of the building of God is indicated by Ephesians 4:16, which says, "All the Body, being joined together and being knit together." All the materials in a building eventually lose their individual identification. Each piece loses its own peculiarity, and every piece becomes the same. A house, for example, is built with many materials. Before each individual, separate, and particular item is built into the house, it is easy to identify because it has its own peculiarity. To be built up, therefore, is to deal with and be delivered from our peculiarities. Whatever is in us that is peculiar needs to be dealt with.

We do not wish to speak concerning this matter in a mere doctrinal way. If we do this, we will only repeat the tragic history of Christianity. Some of the dear saints in the Lord's recovery have the concept that the recovery will grow in a quick way. We can easily hire laborers to pile up materials in a quick way, but we cannot produce a proper building very quickly. In the same way, the Lord's recovery cannot advance quickly, because it is a building, not a movement. If we desire to build up a movement, we can do it quickly, but this will simply be a repetition of the failures of Christianity. There is no need to repeat this history. Rather, we desire to see the saints grow in life and increase in number in all the churches. We do not desire to see a "piling up" of materials; we desire to see the genuine building up. To be built up is to have our peculiarity dealt with. This is not a small matter.

Maintaining a Proper Order in the Body under the Headship of Christ

In addition, every building is something vertical, not only horizontal, and the most useful buildings are the tallest ones. We human beings were not created flat. Only Satan, the serpent, is flat. In principle, every worldly society is a flat serpent, creeping on the dirty earth. Even some of the saints in the Lord's recovery still hold to the concept that the church is "flat," that is, that everyone has the same place in the Body. If we try to make everyone the same in this way, we will turn the church into a serpent. The church is the Body of Christ. A body is not only horizontal but also vertical. For a man to stand vertically indicates that he is strong, but when he is tired, he sits down, and when he is worn out, he lies down. Eventually, when a person is dead, his body lies flat. Too many dear saints still desire the Body to be "flat." This is the subtlety of the enemy. Anything vertical is useful, but whatever is only horizontal loses most of its usefulness. To pull down the pieces of a building and lay them horizontally renders them useless.

To build up something is to cause it to rise up vertically. The more "vertical" a local church is, the stronger it is. Anything that is vertical must have a proper order. The Lord does not set the members in His Body too high or too low. Rather, He has set us all in the proper place (1 Cor. 12:18, 28). If we all remain where we are placed, we will be in the proper order. This is the way of the building. To say that the church is the Body of Christ with the function of all the members does not mean that the members have the same place in the Body. Such a thing would not be the Body. In our physical body, the feet are on the bottom and the head is on top. The feet cannot say, "Head, you are too high; you need to come down. Let us all be the same." Neither can the head say, "Feet, you are too low. Please come up." We hate hierarchy in the church, but we appreciate the headship. Our whole body depends on the head. We may say that a body stands on its feet, but if we would cut off its head, the feet would no longer function. For our body to stand depends very little on the feet. It depends mainly on the head to hold it up. Without the headship, we lose the heading up.

The term *to head up* is not our invention. In Ephesians 1:10 the apostle Paul says, "To head up all things in Christ." In God's creation there was a good order, but by the fall that order was destroyed and humanity became "flat," without the proper headship. From that time until the present and beyond, what God is doing is heading up all things in Christ. Today Christ is our Head, which implies the headship, the authority of the Head over the whole Body. It is the headship of the Head that heads up and holds the entire Body. If we lose the Head, we have no headship, and the Body collapses. In our physical body, every member has its own place in the proper order. The arm is under the shoulder, the hand is under the arm, and the fingers are under the hand. This kind of order maintains the headship, and it is the keeping of the headship that makes the members useful. Once a member loses its position, it is out from under the headship, it is out of function, and it is out of the proper building up. This is not a small matter. It is the problems related to the headship that keep the churches in the Lord's recovery from advancing very quickly.

Many of us have a wrong understanding of the building. If the Lord opens our eyes to see what the proper building is, we will see how short we are of the building up. On the one hand, Christianity throughout the past centuries has rendered much help to us. Even today we are standing on the shoulders of many who have gone before us. On the other hand, Christianity has influenced us in a negative way, and it is very difficult today to lose this influence. If we all mean business with the Lord, we should have a thorough dealing with the

Lord, saying, "Lord, from today I would drop all the doctrinal knowledge, teaching, and practices that I picked up in Christianity and remain in the spirit with You." If we do this, we will be different persons, and our concept will be fully revolutionized.

In the building there must be the proper "vertical" order. Without the proper order, nothing can be built up, and we cannot be useful. This is exactly what the enemy desires. As long as we do not have the building, it makes no difference to him how many meetings we have or how large a crowd we draw. The Roman Catholic Church today has many millions of people all over the world, but since it is the same in principle as any great secular movement in the world, the Lord has no use for it. What the Lord needs is the genuine building. Therefore, we must all pray, look to the Lord for His mercy, and tell Him, "Lord, I need to be built up." This will spontaneously cause us to be radically changed. Those outside the churches do not realize what we are doing here, and they speak all manner of things about us. They understand us only according to what they are and what they practice. Nevertheless, if the Lord has mercy upon us, we will have the proper building up among us.

OUR NEED TO SHEPHERD OTHERS IN OUR DAILY LIFE

In this chapter we will speak concerning our need to shepherd people. To speak about this is difficult, because this matter touches each one of us. To play politics with people is easy, but to touch people in an honest, frank way is not easy. In 1956, when a servant of the Lord visited us in Taiwan, he recommended to us the political way to touch people. He illustrated this way by saying that we should never speak the truth about little babes to their mothers. If a baby is beautiful, we can say, "What a beautiful girl is this!" If the baby is not good looking, however, we should say, "Oh, what a girl this is!" When I heard this, I could not agree with this kind of political speaking. I felt that it was a kind of "British diplomacy." In the Lord's recovery we cannot play politics in this way. If I were here to play politics, there would be no need for the present training.

Shepherding Being
the Most Demanding Need in the Church

The sisters who are mothers know that nothing is as demanding as being a mother. Those who have never had children do not know the real meaning of *demanding*. Nothing and no one in the universe is as demanding as children. If an adult catches a cold, he may not ask for anything, but if a little one has a cold, he must be cared for. A mother can never ask for "sick leave." Even if she is about to die, she must first take care of her child's need. It is the same for fathers. A proper father must take care of his children's demand. A child's demand is without mercy. I have seen many young sisters who could not be adjusted by their father, mother, or even husband, but once they had children, they learned many lessons from these little ones (1 Tim. 2:15). Before they have children, some sisters do not practice to rise early in the morning. It seems that everything in their world is just right for sleeping late. After they have children, however, the little ones wake them up very early. Sometimes when I saw this, I wanted to commend the little children and say, "Very good! What no one else could accomplish for many years, you have done in only a few months." Nothing is as demanding as shepherding, not even gospel preaching. Just as in child raising, everything related to shepherding is not up to us; it is up to the new ones. We cannot say that we have no time or that it is not convenient. This is for those under our care to decide.

Every Member in the Church Having
the Normal Ability to Shepherd People

The way of Christianity is to hire a pastor to shepherd a church. This is not what we mean by shepherding. Some may argue that shepherding is a gift that not every brother or sister has. However, no one would say that raising children is a gift that some have and others do not. Every parent, regardless of how smart or foolish he is, has a talent for raising children. Child raising is not a special talent; it is a talent given by birth. In the same way, by our spiritual birth every member in the church has the gift of shepherding. To say that we do not have the gift of shepherding is to annul our spiritual birth. Some think that because they are too young and are not pastors, elders, or experienced Christians, they cannot shepherd others. This is a wrong understanding and concept. We should forget the wrong teachings we received about shepherding. Someone may not know how to raise children, but when the children come, they are forced to learn. The parents of a young mother may think that she cannot raise her children, but the more they let her do her job, the more she will learn how to do it. We need to drop the wrong concept and pick up the proper one. Even someone who has been saved for only a few days can learn to shepherd.

In order to be the proper, normal members of the church in the Lord's recovery, we need to build up a daily life of the gospel, and we need to go to the Lord for Him to show us who should be under the care of our shepherding. If these two matters are built up in the church, we will have a normal, proper church. A normal church is not merely one in which the members stand to speak something in the meetings. This is only a small part of our service. The main part of the service in the church is a daily gospel life and shepherding. Our concept must be regulated and radically changed. We should realize that it is a great lack and a shame not to bear fruit each year and have someone under our care. All the members in the churches should bear fruit and shepherd people all the time. If we build up these items, the church will be wonderful. The Lord's way is always the best and wisest way. His way is to depend not on spiritual giants but on every member, on those who have a daily gospel life with shepherding. We all need a change of concept in this regard.

More than thirty years ago, I came together every Monday morning with a group of serving ones from 8:00 A.M. until the afternoon to mutually learn how to shepherd people. After meeting for three years in this way, there was a great revival in that locality. This was not due to a movement. It came out spontaneously because of the building up among us. The gospel preaching and the shepherding were adequate and prevailing. This is what the churches need today. The Lord has raised up

His recovery in many cities, but we are still short of a daily gospel living and of shepherding.

FIFTEEN PRACTICAL POINTS CONCERNING SHEPHERDING

Not Being Quick, but Spending an Adequate Amount of Time to Shepherd People

In order to adequately shepherd people, we must not be too quick. Our quick disposition needs to go. We cannot shepherd someone by speaking to them for only a few minutes. Therefore, we must be prepared to spend enough time with people.

Being Positive and Not Sloppy

Although we should not be too quick, we must be very positive. Very often, positive persons are quick ones, and slow persons are passive, even sloppy and uncaring. If a brother says, "Let us go to visit someone," a passive one may say, "We should not be so quick. Let us wait for another two weeks." However, if mothers care for their little ones in this passive way, their children will not survive. We should not be too quick, but we must be positive and on time. The secret of a good surgeon is not to be quick but to be positive and not lose any time. We all need to learn the best way. To this end, we need much work of the cross on our disposition. Anyone can do some amount of shepherding, but to have shepherding that is up to a proper standard, we should be very positive, though not too quick.

Listening to Others in Order to Realize Their True Need and Real Situation

We must learn how to listen to others in order to realize their true need and real situation. This requires us to stop our own thought, concept, feeling, and speaking while we are shepherding them. We should be open to others and allow their situation to speak to us. This is not easy; it means that we must be positive but not quick. We should not say too much or make a decision too quickly. Rather, we should stop ourselves and listen to the person under our care, allowing him to say something, trying our best to understand him, and putting ourselves in his place to understand his situation in the same way as he does.

Many times our visiting damages people rather than helps them. It tears down rather than builds up. This is because we are too raw; we have never been "cooked." Since we have never been dealt with adequately, we are still too wild. As long as we are raw and wild, we are able only to offend people, not to nourish them. Even if we nourish them to a certain extent, we may offend them to a greater extent, resulting in a net debit. We may feel that we have helped a brother, yet we do not realize that we tore him down even more. Eventually, this kind of shepherding produces a loss. Therefore, we all need to be dealt with. Some may say, "In this case, to be a brother or a sister in the local church is too hard. We simply want to go to the meeting on the Lord's Day and enjoy ourselves for an hour by listening to the good singing and speaking. To shepherd people according to a high standard is too great a burden." Yes, this is a burden, but we have no choice. In saying these things, it seems that I am a troublemaker, troubling myself first and then troubling others. However, according to Paul's writings, he was a "troublemaker." He gave himself no peace or rest in his care for the churches (2 Cor. 11:23b-28). He troubled himself, he troubled all the saints, and even today he troubles us. If we read his Epistles, we will all be troubled. The church life is a troubling life, but what other way can we take? We are destined to take this way. As human beings, we must believe in the Lord Jesus, and as believers, we have no choice but to take the way of the proper church life.

Visiting Others without Saying Much

We must also learn not to say too much when we visit people. This is the hardest lesson to learn in shepherding. The longer we wait to say something, the better it is. Someone may ask, "If we should not say anything, why should we contact anyone?" The secret is simply to contact them without saying much. If we speak too much, we will be like the friends of Job. This will waste our time and cause more problems. The best way to shepherd a person is to visit him without saying much. If he asks if we have anything to say, we can simply say, "Praise the Lord. Amen." Over forty years ago some of us would go to Brother Nee and say, "Brother Nee, I have been invited by the church in a certain place. Please tell me what I should do?" He told us, "Do not do anything except this: Whenever they ask you something, you should say, 'I don't know.'" This answer truly bothered us. We said, "If this is the case, we do not need to go. If we do this, they will simply ask us to leave." However, we eventually found that this fellowship rendered us the greatest help.

Because we all assume that we know so much, it is hard to say, "I don't know." Brother Nee taught us to say, "I don't know" because, strictly speaking, we do not know much, and what we do know, we do not know thoroughly. We should not contact people in order to teach them. We ourselves have a greater need of teaching. We should go to the saints and to the churches to learn of them. We must not consider that we know more than they do. It is likely that they know more than we do. Those who went out to the churches without practicing Brother Nee's principle eventually created many problems. The secret to contacting people is not to say much but to let them say something.

Not Making Decisions for Others

We should never make decisions for others. This is to consider that we are superior to them. We should not play politics. We need to be honest with the ones who are under our care, but we must still be restricted by the Lord not to make their decisions.

Never Arguing with People

We also should never argue with people, regardless of whether they are right or wrong. Every conversation is a temptation to adjust others, convince them, or "sell" our good opinions and concepts. We must avoid all these things. There is no need to do this. If we do, it will not help them.

Not Passing On Vain Knowledge

We must never pass on vain knowledge to people. People may ask us about many matters, but we must learn to exercise our spirit to discern the purpose of the questions. If we discern properly, we may realize that the questions are in vain. People often like to gain knowledge, asking about the elders, the brothers and sisters, and many other matters. We must learn to be wise, not be involved with questionings, and not pass on vain knowledge. This also is a difficult lesson for us all.

Not Being Involved in Any Negative Talk

We should not be involved in any negative talk. In other words, we should not be a "trash can." Flies like to find a dirty place, but we must be clean and sterilized. If we do not visit people in a clean way, but rather take germs to them, they may be incited to open up in a wrong way. They will open their "tombs," and death will come out. We should not get into any negative talk or answer any questions about negative matters. We must be in another realm, another kingdom.

Being Honest and Not Political

We must learn to be honest, never pretending and never playing politics. We should not be political in order to make the situation easier. We must be honest persons, answering honestly yes or no. If the situation does not allow us to answer yes or no, then we should not say anything. If we learn all these lessons, we will be able to care for others.

Ministering Life to Others

Most importantly, we must learn to minister life to others. In order to do this, we ourselves must have life. We may illustrate this with money. If we desire to give money to someone, we must first have some ourselves. If our pocket is empty, we have nothing to give. We must have something before we can minister it to others. Therefore, we must learn the lessons of life. Then we will know how to minister to others. In fact, if we have life, there is no need to purposely minister life to others.

Life will already be ministered to them. When visiting others to take care of them, the proper principle is to minister life to them. All the foregoing points are a preparation for ministering life. If we do not have this preparation, whatever we do will only diminish our ministry and supply. If we are careless about any of these matters, our ministry of life will be annulled and swallowed up. If we are careful about all these items, we will remain in a pure condition to minister to others.

Taking the Lead to Bring Others into a Prayer Life

We need to pray with others and help them to pray. We should not try to wrongly impress people that we have the way to do things, that we are smart, or that we know everything. Rather, we should simply help people to put their trust in the Lord and depend on Him for everything. To this end, we should bring with us a spirit and atmosphere of prayer to help others to come into a prayer life. We need to create an atmosphere so that whatever happens to people, they will pray, look to the Lord, and rely on Him for His presence and clear leading. We need to build up those under our care with a prayer life. If we ourselves are not persons with a prayer life, we will not be able to build up others as this kind of person. We ourselves need to take the lead.

Contacting People with Patience

In order to care for others, we need patience. We should not expect that someone who is newly saved or recovered will immediately be in a proper condition. We need patience to care for the weaker ones. A weaker one may require our patience to contact him again and again. This kind of continual, patient contact will shepherd people. This takes time, but there is nothing else we can do. The church grows through shepherding. If we have gospel preaching without shepherding to take care of the new ones, many of the newly saved ones will fall away. This will spoil and damage our appetite for gospel preaching. Many will say, "We brought so many to the Lord, but most of them are not here anymore." We will be like a family that has lost its children. Therefore, we need the proper shepherding for the proper child raising. It is impossible for only the leading brothers in a church to take care of the shepherding. Everyone must pick up the burden to take care of others. This requires our patience.

Trusting Those Who Are under Our Care

We must learn to trust and rely upon the ones who are under our care. This is to have a proper fellowship. In one sense, we are the parents nourishing our children, but in another sense, we are all brothers and sisters. Therefore, we should show others that not only do they rely on us, but we also rely on them. This mutual reliance creates much profit. It causes others to be open to us, trust us, and have confidence in us. This is to "open our veins for the blood to circulate." All the members must be open to one another. Then the circulation will do its proper work. We have seen that some of the ones who are under our care do not open to us, regardless of how much time we spend with them. This means that they have no confidence in us. We need to behave in a way to build up a mutual confidence; this will cause them to open to us. This requires us to depend on them, rely on them, and show them that we need their help.

Never Forcing Anyone to Do Anything

We should never give anyone under our care the sense that we are forcing them to do anything. We must all learn the attributes of God. From the beginning, God never forced people. Rather, He gave them a free choice. We should not even try to overly influence people. Not to force or coerce people is contrary to our natural concept. In shepherding, however, we should stay away from every kind of forcing, coercing, and convincing. We should allow people to have a free choice.

Fellowshipping with Others according to Our Own Experience

Whatever we fellowship with the dear ones must be according to our own experience. Paul told the Thessalonians, "Just as you know how we were to each one of you, as a father to his own children, exhorting you and consoling you and testifying" (1 Thes. 2:11). No doubt, Paul testified many things to the saints, but a great part of his testimony must have been his own experiences. We need personal experiences to be able to testify to the younger ones. In the proper sense, whatever we render to them as a help should be from our own testimony. How much we can testify in this way depends on how much we have experienced. We must have a certain amount of experience of all of the foregoing detailed items. The more we pick up the burden to shepherd others, the more things we will need to learn.

CHAPTER NINE

SHEPHERDING PEOPLE
IN THE EXPERIENCES OF LIFE
FOR THE BUILDING UP OF THE CHURCH

Scripture Reading: 1 Cor. 15:45b; Gal. 2:20; John 15:4; Rom. 8:2, 6, 10; Phil. 3:8-10

In the previous chapter we saw fifteen practical points concerning shepherding. Many of these points covered the things we should not do. We should not go out to contact people with the concept that we can do many things or that we know many things. We must first learn that we can do nothing. If we are truly unloaded in this way, we can go on to learn further matters. In this message we will consider some basic, positive items for our shepherding of others in the church.

SHEPHERDING PEOPLE IN THE EXPERIENCES OF LIFE

Helping People in Each Stage of Life to Have Particular Experiences

We need to shepherd people in the way of experience. This is not simply to share our experiences with them. Rather, when we care for young ones, new ones, and weak ones, we need to know where they are in their experience. We may use the educational system to illustrate the way to help people. If a teacher knows what grades a child has completed, he can help him to advance in a proper way. In the old days in China, those who did not accept the modern educational system would learn only a few things each year in a very general way. By the time they were middle-aged, some still could not write properly. In contrast, all the children in the modern educational system could write well after only a few years. These children learned in the proper way without wasting time. Too many people in Christianity today are not on the proper way. My own mother was baptized and taught in a Christian school when she was young. Because she attended Christian meetings and learned some things there, she was able to tell her children stories from Genesis and the four Gospels. After we were saved, however, we realized that she was not yet saved. She knew many things, but she had no particular experience of salvation. This illustrates our need to help those who are under our shepherding to have definite, particular experiences of life.

We must first know whether someone is clear about the assurance of salvation. Someone may come to the church meetings, but if he is not truly saved, he is not actually in the church. Although we believe that almost everyone in our meetings is saved, some of the new ones who have come into the church life only recently may not have the assurance of salvation. If we check with them, they may say, "I believe I am saved, but I am not very sure." Without the assurance of salvation, it is hard for anyone to go on. Salvation is our foundation, and the assurance of salvation is our motivation. If anyone does not have the assurance that he has been fully saved, it is difficult for him to go on.

If someone is clear concerning his salvation, we should go on from the assurance of salvation to another experience. Perhaps we can help him to have a particular experience of consecration. He is clear about salvation, but he may never have consecrated himself to the Lord. We should not merely pass on a little knowledge about consecration. Instead, we must pray for him, contact him, have fellowship with him, and do something to help him to fully pass through the experience of consecration. Then for eternity he can never say that he has not consecrated himself. To be saved is a particular, initial experience, and following this, people need the assurance of salvation. These are the first two experiences they need. Then we need to help them to pass through a particular, definite, specific experience of consecration. Our ability to do this depends on whether we ourselves have had this experience. After we help people in this way, we can go on to another experience. No doubt, they also need to have a definite experience of clearing their past. In actuality, the clearance of the past and consecration go together.

We must have a particular burden for the new ones. We may realize that a certain brother is very promising but that he has never consecrated himself to the Lord. Then we should not touch this matter in a shallow way. We need to touch this in the deepest way. First we may give him our own testimony and tell him how so many saints in the past consecrated themselves to the Lord. We should contact him several times until we see that he has truly passed through this experience.

After consecration and clearance of the past, we can go on to further experiences. How far we can go with others depends on how far we have gone on. We can help others only to the extent of our own experience. In mathematics, for example, if we have learned only addition and subtraction, this is all that we can teach. If we have had adequate experiences of life, we can help people in a further way. Perhaps we can move on to the inner anointing. To help someone under our care to experience this will take a long time. We need this kind of shepherding, a shepherding according to an "educational system."

I strongly recommend the book *The Experience of Life*. This book was taken from a training course given from 1953 to 1954, which was based on all the experiences of the inner life taught by the saints from the first century. In particular, it relied on a book by Madame Guyon entitled *Life out of Death—Spiritual Torrent*. Mrs. Jessie Penn-Lewis used Madame Guyon's writing very much in her expositions. We received help from both authors, we digested what they spoke, and we added something further. *Spiritual Torrent* is somewhat difficult to understand, but today it is very easy to read *The Experience of Life*. If someone reads from it for ten minutes a day, he can finish the book in a short time. The four stages in the spiritual life mentioned by Madame Guyon are covered in this book, including nineteen experiences of life, and they are presented in a very "scientific" way. Everything related to our physical life can be known scientifically. If we care for our eating, breathing, drinking, working, and resting in a scientific way, we will be healthy. Likewise, we can know the things of the spiritual life in a scientific way. What is presented in *The Experience of Life* is not a mere theory, consideration, or imagination. It is based on the experiences of many seeking saints through the centuries. We should first shepherd ourselves by using this book to check our experience. Doing this will help us to know if we are in "high school," "college," or "graduate school" in our spiritual experience. Then we will know where we are and what our need is.

Knowing the Spiritual Stage of the New Ones in Order to Help Them in a Particular Way

If we do not know where we are or where those whom we contact are, our fellowship with them will be very general. Of course, this is better than nothing, and for the first few contacts this may be good enough. For the long run, however, we need further learning. Then we will know where we are, and we will know where others are. We will know what we are short of, and we will be able to help others to the extent of our own experience. Then the whole church will grow. Otherwise, we will simply meet together in a general way without being clear or knowing what we are doing. Not only the service groups but also every local church with an adequate eldership must help the saints to go on in this way. At first, the church life may be only in the "sixth grade," but after a few years we will advance to "junior high," "high school," and eventually "college." At the same time, some of the new ones will still be in "junior high" and even in "nursery school." As a whole, however, the church will be at a higher level of life. This requires us not merely to give messages week after week. Rather, we must know how to help the saints at every level, just as in America today we have all the different levels of education. Because of this, to be an elder in the proper church life is not an easy burden.

We must all see that this is the proper way of shepherding. Otherwise, we will not be clear what we are doing for the long run. We must know people's spiritual condition. Then we will know where they are and what they need. We will realize whether or not we can afford them what they need, and we will go on to experience something further. This is what it means to shepherd people according to the experiences of life. It is a very definite and particular way. I took this way for many years. At that time, I had no desire to speak concerning other things. I was burdened only to help each one whom I contacted. I would either pray with someone, give a testimony about a particular experience, or read a portion of the Word or a few pages of a book with him. Sometimes I would ask two other brothers to come with me to help a certain person, or I would invite him to dinner for the purpose of helping him. After a few weeks like this, I could see that the new one received a particular and definite help.

We should both bring the new ones into the present flow of the church in a general way and render them the help they need in a particular way. Not all the new ones are able to enjoy whatever the church is enjoying at the present time, although they can enjoy it to some extent. Therefore, we should realize their real situation and discern their real need. Then we can minister to them what they need. The new ones are like the patients of a doctor. They do not know their real condition, but the doctor should know. Then he can determine the kind of dose or treatment they need. Sometimes patients do not understand what the doctor is prescribing to them. A good doctor does not always explain the treatment to people. He may simply give the patient a good-tasting medicine and let it work on the patient. In a general way, we should keep all the saints in the present flow of the church, but in particular, we should know what someone's real need is. Then we can supply that particular need to each particular person.

HELPING PEOPLE TO COME INTO
THE GENUINE EXPERIENCE OF CHRIST

We must always help people to come into the genuine experience of Christ. In principle we all know this, but this is a matter of experience, not of knowing. How much we can help people depends upon how much we have experienced. If we have not experienced much of Christ, we will not be able to help others experience Him. We must all realize that today Christ is the life-giving Spirit (1 Cor. 15:45b). Certain ones advised me not to minister concerning Christ being the life-giving Spirit, saying that people will be offended and not receive it. Nevertheless, I have received a vision from the Lord, and I must tell people that Christ today is the life-giving Spirit. This is not a mere doctrine; it is for people to experience Christ. I was in Christianity for many years, and I heard much talk concerning Christ being our life. However, not many people experience this. If we would ask what people mean by saying that Christ is life, how Christ can be our life, and where Christ is our life, almost no one will be able to answer properly.

In John 15:4, the Lord said, "Abide in Me and I in you." Andrew Murray wrote a book entitled *Abide in Christ*. I read this book, and I have read portions of it several times. This book may be considered a marvelous masterpiece. However, it does not tell us the particular way to abide in Christ. Hudson Taylor also experienced abiding in Christ according to John 15, and we received help from him. Still, our own experience and practice show that without Romans 8, the way to abide in Christ is vague. Romans 8:6 says, "The mind set on the spirit is life and peace." By this we can know who Christ is and where He is. Forty years ago I was groping for the way to experience Christ, but now we have found the "switch" in Romans 8. The way to experience Christ is to build up a habit of remaining in our spirit. We must realize that today our Christ is the life-giving Spirit, the Spirit of life, dwelling in our spirit (vv. 2, 11, 16; 2 Tim. 4:22). This Spirit of life is none other than Christ in us. Now we must have the definite particular experience of living in our spirit, which is life (Rom. 8:10). For many years I knew Galatians 2:20, which says, "It is no longer I who live, but it is Christ who lives in me." However, I did not know how Christ could live in me. The way to experience the Christ who lives in us is by realizing that He is the life-giving Spirit and that we have a human spirit that has been regenerated and enlivened by Christ and with Christ.

There is no limit to this experience. Even when he was older, the apostle Paul still longed to know more of Christ (Phil. 3:8-10). To know Christ and the power of His resurrection is without limitation. More than thirty years ago I received help from a certain elderly sister. When I went to visit her, she testified that something serious had happened to her and that when she went to the Lord to inquire about it, the Lord spoke, "To know Him and the power of His resurrection" (v. 10). The next time I visited her, she testified that something even more serious had happened, but when she went to the Lord to inquire about it, He again spoke the same thing. I received much help and was built up by her testimony. Because she herself had received the experience of Christ as resurrection power, she knew that I was short of it. This was her way of shepherding me. To experience Christ in this way is a great thing.

On the one hand, I am very happy with what the Lord is doing today, but at the same time my heart is aching over the present situation. There are thousands of Christians who know almost nothing about how to experience Christ. They know how to be excited, sing, and praise in a general, emotional, and religious way, but when we try to fellowship with them, we realize that they have little actual experience of Christ. This is the poverty of today's Christianity. We ourselves must not think that we are rich. Whether or not we are rich depends upon how much experience of Christ we have. This is a great need today. We all need to learn the real experience of Christ. Then we will have something solid and rich with which to supply those who are under our care. Otherwise, we are only carrying out a religious work to bring people to the meetings and the service without much of Christ. This is merely a religion, something godly without the presence of Christ, who is the life-giving Spirit in our spirit. This is a great matter that requires our continual exercise.

BEING FOR THE TESTIMONY OF THE CHURCH

The experience of Christ is for the church. Satan is subtle. He may allow us to care for the experience of life, but he would not allow us to properly care for the church. Many times we are foolish in the way we present the church to people. In serving food, we need to know the right time to serve a certain kind of dish. However, most of us do not know whether the church is the main dish, an appetizer, or the dessert.

We often flow like the tide. When we are at "high tide," we damage people by making the church to be everything, but once we realize what we have done, we are at "low tide" and stay away from the matter of the church. God's economy is altogether for the church, but in his subtlety Satan has been and still is deceiving the saints concerning the church. Now we must be clear about the church, and we must know how to fight the battle for the church. With some of the dear ones, we should not speak concerning the church too quickly, but with others, now is the time to tell them about the church. We need to be the good doctors, knowing the right time to administer the dose. To minister concerning the church to the people under our care is not easy. Even if we are able to help people in the experience of Christ as life, if we cannot bring them into the proper church life, we are still short of God's economy.

Brother Watchman Nee fought this battle for years. I observed him for twenty years, from 1932 to the time he was arrested in 1952. In those twenty years he did not receive even one invitation from a denomination. This is because he was absolutely for the church. Today the subtle enemy is doing his best to allow Christians to use Brother Nee's books on life while hiding what he said about the church. Brother Nee pointed out to us that God's light was with us in those days simply because we were on God's way. If we had been off of God's way, we would have lost the right angle to see the light. The light comes from the direction of God's way. Many denominational leaders asked, "Why does that 'little flock' always receive light? When they open to any page of the Bible, light comes out. Why did we not see the light first instead of receiving it from them?" Brother Nee's secret was that he was on the Lord's way and direction. However, although he always had the light, he suffered persecution. If Brother Nee were here today in the United States, he would be the biggest target of opposition. Many of his appraisers would turn into opposers.

We are here not for any other testimony; we are here for the testimony of the church. This is a real battle. How much we are able to minister to people concerning the church life depends on how much we have experienced. We need to know the reality, ground, history, and destiny of the church. All these require us to learn and to have a certain amount of experience.

BUILDING UP OTHERS IN THE CHURCH LIFE

Building Up the Members in Their Function

We must all know how to build up the church. We should not be too proud and think that only we can build up others, nor should we be too humble and think that only others can build us up. We need to be built up, and we need to build up others. The genuine building up of the church includes several items. First, to build up the church we must help people to function. This is a great need, because without functioning there is no building up. In Christianity there is not much real building; there is mainly organization. We need to help people to function so that they may be built up. If someone never takes the opportunity to function in the church life, he can never be built into the church. He needs us to build him up in his function. This is a part of our shepherding.

Building Up Others in Daily Gospel Preaching

For the building up of the church, we also need the proper daily gospel preaching. This is why we must emphasize this matter. This should not be something that we merely give messages about. It must be something that we all get into, and we must build up others in this. This is the responsibility not only of the elders but of all of us. We all need to be built up in the daily gospel life. Then we can build up others in this way. This is a difficult job, but it is crucial to the building up of the church.

In the past, certain Christian groups had a certain amount of spirituality, but due to their lack of a gospel-preaching life, many of those groups came to nothing. They became like old people without children. Even in the human life, it makes a great difference whether we have children, especially as we grow older. In order to have a proper life, we all need children. In the church life, we need a daily addition of new believers. If one new believer were added to the church each day, we would all be very living. On the other hand, if not one new believer is added to the church in six months, the whole church life will decline. This would indicate that we are wrong, and in this condition it will be impossible to have a proper church life. Whether we have new ones is a test to our church life, indicating clearly whether we are hot or cold. We need a gospel-preaching daily life. This does not require us to do nothing but zealously preach the gospel day and night. Instead, we simply need to help the saints to be built up in their daily gospel preaching.

Building Up Those under Our Care to Also Care for Others

We also need to help the ones under our care to learn how to take care of others. Even if they were only recently saved, they can still care for others. Everyone in the church life is a caretaker. We are all doing the work of shepherding. We do not need one person to "pastor" the church; the church shepherds itself. To build up people to care for others is a great work.

Building Up Others to Know the Church

We must also help people to know the church. To build people up in the foregoing four ways—to function, to have a daily gospel-preaching life, to shepherd others, and to know the church—requires us to have much exercise.

Because we are lacking in the proper building up, many sisters do not use their time well. The sisters in the church should have carried out certain things, but they have not. This is because they do not know how to shepherd people in the experience of life. Even after a long time, someone under the care of the sisters may receive only a general help but nothing in a particular way. A few years ago the one being cared for may not have had certain particular experiences, but today she may still not have had them. The only difference is that now she has learned something in a merely doctrinal way. The ones caring for her have passed on only knowledge to her.

Many times we have charged the saints not to come together to gossip but to speak concerning spiritual things or pray. We thank the Lord that many dear ones have taken this word. However, if we do not know how to shepherd people in the experiences of life, we will not have much to speak of when we come together. At first we can say, "Let us pray-read something," but after doing this a few times, it will not be very prevailing. If we stay on the line of the experiences of life, we will never be short of anything to speak of. We will be like proper school teachers, knowing what "grade" people are in and what we should give them. Otherwise, after contacting one another day after day, we will still remain the same.

The fellowship in this chapter should give us an impression of what our real need is. This is why in the proper church life we need to spend some time to have a training, not simply church meetings. Because the church meetings are too general, it is difficult to carry out a particular training in the meetings. The elders need to pick up the responsibility to build up the saints in the foregoing four basic items—the stages of the experience of life, the enjoyment of Christ, the testimony of the church, and building up the church. I hope that the elders will bring this matter to the Lord and take time to consider how to keep the church on this line. Otherwise, we will be like today's Christianity.

THE ESSENTIAL, BASIC ELEMENTS
OF PROPER SHEPHERDING

No shepherding can be prevailing if we do not have a love for people, an interest in them, a burden for them, and adequate prayer. Love, interest, burden, and prayer are the essential, basic elements of proper shepherding. Most of us were born with no interest in people. We do not like people, and we do not wish to be bothered by them, invited by them, or visited by them. We would rather live on top of a mountain. This is our natural tendency. However, if we keep this kind of disposition, we will be finished with the building. We need to love the new ones as the Lord loves them, be interested them, and take care of them. Then we must have a burden for them and adequate prayer. In addition, the fifteen practical points concerning shepherding in the previous chapter are very useful. We need to be patient, know how to deal with people, and know what to say and what not to say. We should know how to be positive yet not too quick, not for our sake but for the ones who are under our care. Our basic need, however, is love, interest, burden, and prayer. If we would practice all these things, the church will grow in a proper way and be built up under the hands of all the saints, not only the elders or those with a special ministry. Everyone in the service groups in the church life must build up the church. There is no need to depend wholly upon the elders. Sometimes the elders cannot do the job adequately; therefore, we must all take up some part of the work of shepherding. Then the church will receive the benefit. Although it would be better to have a training on these matters all year round, what we have shared here should still give an impression of what we need to practice for the normal way of fruit-bearing and shepherding for the building up of the church.

.

About the Author

Witness Lee was born in 1905 in northern China and raised in a Christian family. At age 19 he was fully captured for Christ and immediately consecrated himself to preach the gospel for the rest of his life. Early in his service, he met Watchman Nee, a renowned preacher, teacher, and writer. Witness Lee labored together with Watchman Nee under his direction. In 1934 Watchman Nee entrusted Witness Lee with the responsibility for his publication operation, called the Shanghai Gospel Bookroom.

Prior to the Communist takeover in 1949, Witness Lee was sent by Watchman Nee and his other co-workers to Taiwan to ensure that the things delivered to them by the Lord would not be lost. Watchman Nee instructed Witness Lee to continue the former's publishing operation abroad as the Taiwan Gospel Bookroom, which has been publicly recognized as the publisher of Watchman Nee's works outside China. Witness Lee's work in Taiwan manifested the Lord's abundant blessing. From a mere 350 believers, newly fled from the mainland, the churches in Taiwan grew to 20,000 in five years.

In 1962 Witness Lee felt led of the Lord to come to the United States, settling in California. During his 35 years of service in the U.S., he ministered in weekly meetings and weekend conferences, delivering several thousand spoken messages. Much of his speaking has since been published as over 400 titles. Many of these have been translated into over fourteen languages. He gave his last public conference in February 1997 at the age of 91.

He leaves behind a prolific presentation of the truth in the Bible. His major work, *Life-study of the Bible,* comprises over 25,000 pages of commentary on every book of the Bible from the perspective of the believers' enjoyment and experience of God's divine life in Christ through the Holy Spirit. Witness Lee was the chief editor of a new translation of the New Testament into Chinese called the Recovery Version and directed the translation of the same into English. The Recovery Version also appears in a number of other languages. He provided an extensive body of footnotes, outlines, and spiritual cross references. A radio broadcast of his messages can be heard on Christian radio stations in the United States. In 1965 Witness Lee founded Living Stream Ministry, a non-profit corporation, located in Anaheim, California, which officially presents his and Watchman Nee's ministry.

Witness Lee's ministry emphasizes the experience of Christ as life and the practical oneness of the believers as the Body of Christ. Stressing the importance of attending to both these matters, he led the churches under his care to grow in Christian life and function. He was unbending in his conviction that God's goal is not narrow sectarianism but the Body of Christ. In time, believers began to meet simply as the church in their localities in response to this conviction. In recent years a number of new churches have been raised up in Russia and in many eastern European countries.

OTHER BOOKS PUBLISHED BY
Living Stream Ministry

Titles by Witness Lee:

Abraham—Called by God	0-7363-0359-6
The Experience of Life	0-87083-417-7
The Knowledge of Life	0-87083-419-3
The Tree of Life	0-87083-300-6
The Economy of God	0-87083-415-0
The Divine Economy	0-87083-268-9
God's New Testament Economy	0-87083-199-2
The World Situation and God's Move	0-87083-092-9
Christ vs. Religion	0-87083-010-4
The All-inclusive Christ	0-87083-020-1
Gospel Outlines	0-87083-039-2
Character	0-87083-322-7
The Secret of Experiencing Christ	0-87083-227-1
The Life and Way for the Practice of the Church Life	0-87083-785-0
The Basic Revelation in the Holy Scriptures	0-87083-105-4
The Crucial Revelation of Life in the Scriptures	0-87083-372-3
The Spirit with Our Spirit	0-87083-798-2
Christ as the Reality	0-87083-047-3
The Central Line of the Divine Revelation	0-87083-960-8
The Full Knowledge of the Word of God	0-87083-289-1
Watchman Nee—A Seer of the Divine Revelation ...	0-87083-625-0

Titles by Watchman Nee:

How to Study the Bible	0-7363-0407-X
God's Overcomers	0-7363-0433-9
The New Covenant	0-7363-0088-0
The Spiritual Man 3 volumes	0-7363-0269-7
Authority and Submission	0-7363-0185-2
The Overcoming Life	1-57593-817-0
The Glorious Church	0-87083-745-1
The Prayer Ministry of the Church	0-87083-860-1
The Breaking of the Outer Man and the Release ...	1-57593-955-X
The Mystery of Christ	1-57593-954-1
The God of Abraham, Isaac, and Jacob	0-87083-932-2
The Song of Songs	0-87083-872-5
The Gospel of God 2 volumes	1-57593-953-3
The Normal Christian Church Life	0-87083-027-9
The Character of the Lord's Worker	1-57593-322-5
The Normal Christian Faith	0-87083-748-6
Watchman Nee's Testimony	0-87083-051-1

Available at
Christian bookstores, or contact Living Stream Ministry
2431 W. La Palma Ave. • Anaheim, CA 92801
1-800-549-5164 • www.livingstream.com